Lifes-lessons

All we have to do is be open to receive...

Joseph A. Drolshagen

Life's-lessons
All we have to do is be open to receive...

ISBN-13: 978-1519382818
ISBN-10:1519382812

www.josephadrolshagen.com
ifgtcoahcing@gmail.com
Facebook:
    Joseph A. Drolshagen
Twitter: Lifeslessons00

For my Mom

FOREWORD

In my years of being a Breath worker and experiencing the power of the breath, it is truly an honor to go on a journey of awakening with someone. Usually that person really has no idea what they are in for if they fully commit to utilizing this healing and awakening modality. Usually there is an energetic withhold and wall to overcome. However, it was not that way with Joseph, many times his awareness came at the speed of light. Many times, his questions were way beyond what I had expected. He was moving on and out from his old thought patterns, and once releasing the energy that trapped them, he would have great and profound insight as to how it all worked. What once took someone months or years to come into acceptance about, Joseph would process and awaken to within days. When he started putting his life's journey into writing, it became an inspiration to me and many others, and he assisted anyone who would listen. His was, and is, a heartfelt leap into opening up a completely new world. His appetite for new pathways to open up became a driving force. His healing that came about as he wrote the daily blog transitioned into a sort of therapeutic writing; it gave way to a Soul coming about. To merge with the higher aspect of self and allows that aspect to step forward. That part of Joseph shows up every time he posts from his heart,

telling us all how he went from THINKING from his Head, to LIVING from his Heart.
I am so grateful for the opportunity to share my love of breath work, Soul awakening with Joseph. His writing here clearly spells out the journey we all travel, and on that journey, we meet our true selves.

Paula Rowe
Founder of Soul Awakening Project
Breath worker
Espira Method of Breathwork teacher
Soul Coach
St. Clair Shores, MI

Recognition

This book could not have been possible had it not been for the burning desire of my spirit within; whom I consider me Higher Power!

To my Mom & Dad. Even when you did not understand what the heck, I was saying in my blog posts, you continually asked me to read them to you. You have given me such an awesome example of a love story between the two of you and I'm proud to have you both as role models... May you both rest in peace and love!
To my son, Joey. You taught me about unconditional love. I am so grateful to be your dad. *To my friends Kevin, Blair, Patrick & Brian.* You helped me step into true manhood, and continue to be the other half of "iron sharpens iron."
To all my teachers I have met throughout my life who have taught me lessons, even when I did not appreciate the person or the lesson!
To Paula. Teaching and coaching me, Rebirth Breathwork has opened the doors into a level of existence I could not even imagine prior! *To Annette Rochelle Aben.* Without "your kick in the pants", this book would still be a bucket list item!

And to Julie... My greatest teacher...

Introduction

I have spent a majority of my life as a seeker. This is how I would best describe myself. A twisty, swerving, bumpy, pounding, hilly road of seeking. I have by no means been *angel-like*; although, I have known all my life how *good* feels. I have felt a constant throughout my life for this internal need to understand who God is and where I am in relation.

At twelve (12- years- old, my father told me I had to toughen up. I did not know to ask what he meant, and he did not know to be clear about that.
Immediately after that conversation, I began practicing becoming red hot angry. It encouraged me to spend my teen years fighting. The larger impact to me was in that moment of decision, a twelve (12)-year-old child took on and lived out a belief that he was not good enough as he was. Over time I realized what my Dad was telling me back then. That I was too sensitive.

Today... I ask questions! Lots of them!! One of my favorite sayings is, "There is never a bad question."

I have spent a large portion of the past eighteen (18) years working on, studying and growing spiritually, emotionally and physically. I have studied Christianity to Buddhism, and am working with a

Master Breath worker, who I consider to be a teacher as well as my friend (*Paula Rowe, Soul Awakening Project*).

I continue to be a student of various forms of meditation and although **www.lifes-lessons.com** is my first publication, I have tablet upon tablet of writings that have assisted me in better understanding who that twelve (12)-year-old boy was, and why he was perfect just as he was.

Today, I work on feeling who I am, not thinking. Being, not doing. All the great teachers I follow speak of this. Shutting off the mind and feeling direction. This shift from thinking to feeling has had an amazing impact on my life! It excites the hell out of me, and I want so much to share this and be in community with others who are on this journey.

The purpose of my blog **www.lifes-lessons.com**, and this book, is to bring to light that everything we experience is a lesson for us in which to learn. This book is built on chronological events in my life as they unfolded. I hope that through reading these events and their overall lessons, the reader will start asking simple questions of himself or herself.

What if...

There was no such thing as judgement

No right and no wrong

No good and no bad

No fair or unfair

And if everything happens for our benefit...

"WHY IS THIS HAPPENING IN MY LIFE?"

That question has literally changed my life!

Namaste and many Blessings to you my friend, Joseph.

Lessons Learned in Life... Trust

 Today, I find myself looking at TRUST. What it really means and how I apply it. Or not! I have always considered myself a trustworthy guy.

 About a month ago, I had a shirt missing from my closet. It is the *go-to* shirt my girlfriend Julie wears whenever she visits because she states that, "I'm cheap and don't like the turn the furnace up," she says. When I realized the shirt was missing, I called her and was adamant that she took it home. I told her I would need it back. I knew without a doubt that she took it. 'Maybe not on purpose' was how I framed it, so I was not coming right out and calling her the thief. My screwed-up thinking thought she could be. Well, I found the shirt in a duffle bag in my basement. When I did, I called her and apologized.

 Lesson one, right? NOPE... needed more examples!

 The other day, my son, Joey returned home from school in his usual manner, which meant, he relaxed in front of the TV for a bit. I noticed he had a set of ear buds for his phone. I remember mine were hanging from my mirror in my bedroom and went

1

to get them to make sure I packed them for my upcoming hunting trip. Guess what… Yep, you guessed it, THEY WERE GONE! I told (notice I did not say *asked*) Joey they were mine, to which he replied, "No, they are not". I was so adamant that the ear buds were mine, and so angry I was swearing and saying things that I am embarrassed to repeat. I accused him of taking my things. Five minutes or so into this heated conversation, a quick thought ran through my head reminding me of my reaction to the shirt incident. I sat for a minute and breathed deeply
to reduce the adrenaline that comes with a good old' fashion anger surge, but also to let the shirt event permeate enough for me to be willing to believe something different. As a result, I told Joey I didn't believe he took my ear buds and asked if he would help me find them, which he did. They were in my luggage. I probably packed them earlier in the day.

I continue to have events unfolding to help me see how untrustworthy I have actually been throughout my life, for example, when new sales people come into the picture at work, my reaction is to protect my territory against their invasion. Or another example: I have a change jar that I have locked, to the point, that it is a "pain in the butt" to use. Instead, I put my change on a dresser, scattered all over the place. I probably lose more change now than anyone would ever take!

My lesson in all this, after apologizing and "coming clean" with Joey and Julie was that there is something inside of me who believes people are "out to take" from me. As this unfolds, I see more and more areas of my life where I acted from this belief, causing ill feelings to myself and others. I expect I am blocking myself from fully receiving because I have spent so much time guarding and protecting. I realize I have been trustworthy as long as I have all my things inventoried and accounted for. BUT I can become trustworthy as events happen in my life to help me practice becoming so. Once again, I cannot expect to grow in this life unless I am willing to look honestly at where I am.

Lessons Learned in Life: Acceptance

Today's words of encouragement come with the "kicked in the kahunas" kind of feeling!

I spent most of this past weekend feeling the exact opposite of Acceptance. This seems to be an ongoing lesson in my life, with new events regularly evolving in order to allow me to continue learning.

To start with a little background, from the time my son was old enough to walk, until he was too old to enjoy it, we would take one week every year for a "Man Trip" which ranged from camping, to traveling to different places. Renting an airplane and flying to an airport fifteen (15) minutes away and spend hours playing football (off the airstrip, of course) and talking. I found airports that were only fifteen (15) minutes away because he never has liked long trips, so I would keep the trips short enough so he might not complain. Heck, he is still the only person I have ever spent the night with at a Bed and Breakfast. We were scolded for wrestling in the room... My goal has always been for us to be very close.

In 2007 I moved to Wisconsin for a job and the

plan was for the family to move. A few months into it, my wife and I started divorce proceedings. I was four states away from my son. I spent the next year in fear of never being able to do things with him, and every week, I traveled to Michigan after work on Friday to spend Saturday 10:00 am until Sunday 8:00 pm with him. I would drive back to Wisconsin in time for work Monday morning.

The memory of this time period, breaks me all over again to write about it! I took a lesser position and moved back to Michigan in 2008, and started a yearlong battle for 50% custody, which through a miracle, I was granted (truly amazing story that I hope I find an avenue to share here sometime).

My son will be eighteen (18) years-old in April. He has decided he wants to live full time at his mother's house. As any decent parent who has felt that special gratitude to be trusted to assist in raising one of God's children, I have spent the past eighteen (18) years doing what I honestly believe to be the best I am able to; love him, be close with him, and to make sure he has the tools to face life. Very similar to the model I grew up with, I have taken on the role of the tougher, stricter parent. But at the same time, I have been the wrestling, game playing, hockey coaching, jokester who spent every morning I have had him, trying to make him laugh before school.

So now, I am faced with the decision about what to do with all the feelings that resulted from this conversation. The feelings of rejection, anger, the *poor me*, and if I am going to be rigorously honest, 'The Victim'. All the studies I have read, teach me I should instantly kick into remembering that, 'Nothing is good, nor bad' and 'Everything that happens to me is for my benefit/growth" or I could remember, 'I am complete and whole, regardless of and/all outside influences". I did not remember any of these phrases until the past several hours. I did spend Friday night, all of Saturday and most of Sunday feeling hurt, angry, resentful and sorry for myself.

Around 3:00 A.M. Monday morning, I started to remember... As soon as I was tired of feeling the way I was, the moment I hurt enough to relinquish control of the world being MY WAY, I asked for help. Somewhere deep inside of my chest area was a feeling with the words, "It's OK. It's OK EXACTLY as it is. Life is changing, and it isn't good or bad. It just is." This morning that feeling is growing into realizing I have done a great job teaching him how to be a man! He did not run

to his mom to ask her to tell me, or find some way to cause me to push him away. He looked me straight in the face and told me what he wanted and needed. I have said all along that I feel like he teaches me more than I do him. I respect and admire him for the person he is today!

Lessons Learned in Life: Gratitude

In the spirit of the season (and maybe due to the first good night's sleep I have had in three days) it seems fitting to take a minute and talk about how blessed I am. Hence G-R-A-T-I-T-U-D-E! Not just for the overflowing abundance that I see, touch and feel whenever I choose to see, such as the past lessons of my life and what they have taught me. And I am not necessarily referring to money or material things, although I consider myself very fortunate and blessed in this arena as well. I am learning that material and money are good fortunes that I am supposed to enjoy and take delight in while I walk my path on this beautiful planet, but I want to write about that later.

What I am referring to is this feeling I have within my chest. This feeling of faith I carry in my heart is knowing that my "vibration" or "my knowledge of who I really am" is growing richer. I actually have a deep, energetic gratitude for what can be. I am not sure about anyone who is reading this, but for me, to have even a good feeling about the future is an awesome gift!

"How did I get this feeling" one might ask. Or not. But either way I'm writing about it! It seems the more I make my decision to feel grateful in the moment, the more faithful I am about expecting the future to continue to bestow blessing upon me and life lessons to guide me. I have to believe the things I am focusing on, such as self-discovery, meditation and recovery are led to the awareness of my increasing level of vibration with the One. I am finding the One is everything, and includes all of us. The gratitude is my willingness to be a participant in discovering me, and ultimately finding God. While recently reviewing some of my personal writings, I came across one where I wrote,

"I set out seeking God, in doing so I found myself, which I ultimately found to be one and the same."

I remember becoming aware of this. It came with an awe! I realize that God is so much more than some sort of higher being up in the sky, or a superior entity deciding the fate or destination of my life. I am a "cup of the ocean" that is Him. I think about that and how can it mean anything other than, I am Him? A part of Him? "I am He & He is I." I believe it is the same for all of us. This belief is the roots of my gratitude.

My gratitude is in knowing I have never been nor ever will be limited by anyone or anything outside myself. That the only thing that has ever held me from having the perfect life (as I get to define it) is my misunderstanding of who I am. And if that is correct, then all I have to do is be honest with myself and be open for the events and people who come into my life; what they have to teach me as well as learn from me. It is always there at the perfect time for me to rediscover who I am. WOW!

Lessons Learned in Life: EGO

Up until recently, I spent the past few years raising a beagle. Rudy was such a great dog. I felt it necessary to find another home for him a few months ago because of how much travel I do for work. Since he left, come to think of it, I have not seen any rabbits in the backyard. They used to be scurrying all over the yard, just outside his fence, like they were intent on tormenting Rudy.

Anyway, a while back Rudy snuck out of the yard and took off, which he liked to do as often as possible. I have found him at the police department on several occasions because of the weak batteries in his collar. But this particular time, it was about ten in the morning when I realized he escaped. I went into the woods behind the house and called for him for about an hour with no return sound from him. In disgust, I returned to the house and went back to work. One of those times when I would wish I could hear his howl, but I was angry with him all at the same time.

About three o'clock I heard him bark. I walked into the yard and heard him again. I followed his bark and started calling him, which he returned by continuing to bark. I followed his voice through the woods, weed and thickets to find him chained to a garage. I saw he had food and water in bowls within his reach and instantly made a decision that these people were stealing my dog. I remember that feeling of heat and anger rising within me, and I remember asking myself if I should go to the door and punch whomever answers it.

 I do not think I purposely took deep breaths to better assess the situation, but I am thinking I must have. At least enough of a pause to allow the thought, "If you're not sure what to do Joe, do not do anything." I still remember internally agreeing with this thought, and I also thought that if I was supposed to punch someone, I could easily come back in the near future and do so. So, I untied Rudy and brought him home and put him in his kennel, so I could attend a meeting.

 At the meeting I discussed this event because it is one of the first times, I can remember not taking an action when I did not know what action to take. Which really meant I did not make a bad situation worse! I also was not sure if I owed someone a good ol' fashion butt

XXXhopping', so I was looking for feedback on that as well. What I received was feedback from two different people after the meeting closed. They both asked me if I ever thought of thanking the person, who for all practical purposes, stopped Rudy from being run over, since in front of their house is a busy mile road, with a fifty (50) mile an hour speed limit. Both times I said, honestly, "NO, I didn't think about that." I was only focused on someone taking something from me. This is where I experienced the EGO deflation. I did not feel a need to lie and I did not feel negative about myself. I just did not know and there was no more judgment than that. I remember thinking, 'Oh, I didn't think of that'. Both people and I laughed, and I thanked them for helping me to see this other option.

The next day I did go to the neighbor and thanked him. I did not feel it necessary to share with him how close he came to receiving the wrath of Joe because I am gifted with having an arena where I can share who I am and have close enough friends to give me input. The other reason I did not feel it necessary to share how close this tough looking dude came to getting punched is because I thought he could probably wipe the streets with me!

Lessons Learned in Life... Perspective

Sometimes I feel that life is hard.

Then I received a call from a close friend, telling me her Mom just died.

My troubles automatically seemed trivial.

These are my words of wisdom for today.

Lessons Learned in Life: Reality

Reality. It took my Mom falling and breaking her hip, and spending the night with her at the hospital, waiting to see if her heart was strong enough for her to make it through surgery for me to hear the story about her and my Dad having a cherry pit spitting contest not long ago.

What an amazing love story!

They just celebrated 51 years of marriage.

Lessons Learned in Life: Practice

Today, I spent the day practicing. It seems the days I work on practicing some small aspect of life, the more I feel in tune with the ultimate energy force around me. I recognize the more I have this outlook, the more loving I feel towards myself and others.

I have a friend of mine who used to tell me "the most overlooked word in the entire dictionary, with regards to living a healthy life, is the word practice". I have also heard, "Practice these principles in all our affairs". In taking time to ponder this thought, I could make the argument that our entire existence is about practice. I reach out, open up, learn, become aware, or however I choose to describe the insights that flow to me. The next step is to either disregard the information, or to start practice implementing it into my life.

For me, more and more of my life becomes practice, for instance, I continue practicing healthy eating habits. I think this is an area I struggle with on a regular basis. Every day I wake up with the intention of going to bad that night knowing I treated my body the way I want others to treat me. In my past, a bad day of eating lead me so miserable about who I am, all based on what I ate or did not eat, that I would eat again to take away the pain I created.

Here is what I have found for myself with regards to practicing anything...

Ultimately, everything I practice is love, or the lack of love. In order for me to practice anything in love, I have to do so WITHOUT judgment! Anytime I use judgment in my practices, I've lost. It took me a while to be able to put aside good or bad, right or wrong, success or failure, in order to be enough, just being ME.

It seems from my experience that the more I realize I'm practicing life, the deeper understanding I receive that I am never going to be perfect. This means where I am right now, in this second, is as close to perfect as I can get.
How awesome of a thought is that? Really?! Not only is there no judgment in it, but it frees me of any negativity towards myself. I have actually thought to myself, "If I was as close to perfection yesterday while doing so and so, how much closer must I be doing this."

When I realize the full impact of this thought, I automatically want to eat healthier, regardless of whatever I have done up until this point. I want to ask for help from others, without feeling like I am weak for doing so. I want to keep going forward because I know I can. Practicing life is SOOOOO much easier than performing it "right."

I am not saying that by removing judgment and looking at life as practicing will bring my weight down to 185 pounds. What I am saying is that looking at life as a practice helps me to remove judgment. And by removing judgment, I feel more love (motivation) to "Be." And by 'Being" is how mountains are moved...

I hope whomever reads this can take one item from his or her life today, something that has been causing guilt, shame, sadness or unhappiness of any kind, and practice one thing different with regards to it. If you are practicing, you will understand that you are perfect exactly as you are in this moment. And you understand if the outcome is not a homerun today, that you are at batting practice preparing to experience seeing the ball disappearing into the stands, and you WILL have your chance to do the slow run around the bases.

We all do. It is the plan for each of us. All we have to do is believe, bask in this moment, and keep on practicing!

Lessons Learned in Life: Time

Today's subject, Time, originated earlier in the week. It has been coming to me for years, but for whatever reason today is the day it made its way into my awareness. And like most of my lessons, it came to me without my realizing it was going to impact a change and understanding in my life.

Earlier this week I was talking on the phone and the subject was a three-year-old child. In the discussion we talked about how at that age, children have no concept of time.
Everything is either now or later. To try to explain something will happen at 8:00 pm Monday, or noon on Saturday means nothing to them. They do not comprehend the days of the week, hours or minutes (unless time-out is applied). They do not care which meal description fits into which part of the day. They know they are hungry and need to eat. What they know is NOW. Play now, eat now, watch their favorite show now, wrestle now, snuggle now. They spend as much of their time living in the now as parents allow.

I think my lesson has to do more with applying balance in my life than with being able to explain

21

the difference between carefree and disciplined; although I do believe the difference between a child and an adult is conditioning. I have made decisions in my life to read books such as "**The One Minute Manager**", and "**Effective Time Management**". I chose to work as a program manager for quite a few years in my career. This meant I was responsible to build timelines and manage teams to meet the milestones.

Without my buy-in and definitely without realizing what I was ultimately doing to myself, I set out on a course of living my life in a rigid disciplined manner. An event happened to me two years ago that explains this perfectly. I was traveling out of town with someone and she had the audacity to want to go shopping as soon as we left the arriving airport grounds. What the freak is this?!?! Any decent, seasoned traveler, such as myself, knows upon arriving someplace, the first step is ALWAYS to check into the hotel. That is what you do! And there are very good reasons for doing so! The second step is to unpack. Unpacking consists of hanging up hanger-clothes, taking clothes out of luggage and placing them in drawers that almost every hotel includes in their price. Finally, yet no less important than the first two, is arranging toiletries in the bathroom. If there is more than one person, the counter needs to be sub-divided to accommodate for everything.

Heck, I am even Ok if it's not an even 50/50 split. Then and only then can things, such as, shopping, eating or any other activity be discussed. There is no other way!! OK, there is one thing I could be convinced to put in between checking into the hotel but before unpacking.

Well, I lost and my decision was not the popular one we went with. For the first half hour that we were shopping I felt irritated, ticked off and thought that I was the only adult on this trip. Once I explained why I felt the way I did and realized how silly it seemed to be upset over this, we went shopping, out to lunch and had a blast. Once we finally checked into the hotel, I was even able to joke about being as bothered as I was, but I wondered why my emotions felt so tightened by this. I have been unable to figure out the answer to that question until today.

Earlier today, I had the privilege of a day hike in Crowder Mountain, SC. I am so grateful I have opportunities like this in my life. It was supposed to be 5.2 miles, but I do not think it would be exaggerating for me to say I strung it out to six (6) miles. Not on purpose, but because I was trying to participate in a conference call for work and still hike, so I turned when I should have gone straight. The hike required rock climbing. Not cliffs, but high enough that I was excited about my accomplishment! This climbing forced my mind to focus on where I was more than any of the chattering thoughts that can consume my time.

The conference call went well and after I figured out which direction I was supposed to be heading, I again realized the beautiful surroundings, the sound of a light wind rustling the few remaining leaves that still hung from trees. The ideal weather, brisk enough to keep a guy my size from overheating, yet not cold enough to push me to a running pace...lol I felt really calm and into the moment. I felt satisfied right in the moment.

Then I felt this overwhelming feeling of weightlessness go through my entire being. I felt as though I was floating through the trail rather than hiking, as if gravity lost most of its pull on me. I felt this feeling that if I didn't hear the leaves crunching under my feet, I would have bet I was floating. I was moving uphill, downhill, changing direction from right to left, depending on where the trail led completely effortlessly. I didn't feel like I have at times when I am on a spiritual high. It was much calmer than that. It was more being a part of. Being moved as opposed to moving. There was no outside thought, just this awed, calm, peaceful feeling. After what I would guess to be an hour or so, I remember having a quick thought of wondering what time it was. I remembered that I had to check out of my hotel by 1:00 and all of a sudden, SWOOSH! Everything I was feeling immediately vanished. At first, I tried to forget about checking out of my hotel, but I could not. So, I checked my watch and found I had seventy-five (75) minutes to get back, shower, pack and check out. I fought off the thoughts about packing, which consisted of shoes, then hanger-clothes, then remainder, with toiletries on top. For the remainder of the hike I could not get that feeling of weightlessness back.

So, for my lesson... since I live in the world, I do need some areas of structure to accomplish the goals that are important to me. But I do not need even a fraction of what I have subjected myself to throughout my adult life. I realize that I need to be aware of the areas that call for me to be child-like.
Finally, I need to make darn sure I regularly have unstructured time available for me *to be.* I laugh because my first thought is to set many hours per week to be unstructured...lol Even as I laugh at this, I know this would be a start, if it is all I can do. Knowing the days of the week, being able to tell time and having the knowledge and

ability to bring structure seems to be more crippling than healthy, in the manner I have applied it. I am sure it all depends on application. I shall find out!

Lessons Learned in Life: Faith

I used to think God moved in and out of my life, depending on what I was doing, or how "good" I was, how faithful I was, or how unselfish I was. I am learning how crippling this way of thinking is to me, my spirituality, and even my earthly relationship

I have heard for a long time, sayings like, "God doesn't move, we do." It makes sense to me, but I do not think until recently I realized the depth of this statement. During a conversation with my Dad, it sank in, how encompassing it is throughout my entire life.

We had been talking about my Dad's cancer, which had returned; his frustration, depression and fear over it all. During the conversation I asked him where God was in his life. He told me he had not spoken to God since the cancer returned. He felt left behind by God...

That made me think, hence my lesson...

I start out being the best me I can in whatever situation I am in. We all do. I decide everything about everything through my programming and

how I see the world. I do my very best to be a good person and my way of living. I make the best possible decisions I can and during it all, my ego convinces me of what a great man I am. I went as far as I could living this way. Eventually I crashed!
This applies to all of life, as well as individual situation I have encountered.

So, I began work at building a strong relationship to whatever I consider God to be. We do this for various reasons. I know for myself, I did so because I ran my life so far into negativity and depression that I had to find an entirely new way of living, or giving up completely During this phase I lived my life by what 'I THINK.'

I now have this awesome relationship that brings new insights, a new discovery of who I am in relation to the world, miracles galore, and I am on top of the world.
Ultimately, what we are doing is opening ourselves to being directed, or guided through our path by a higher power (God). I open myself to 'THY WILL' and miracles start happening within my life as a regular occurrence. 'Miracles' being coincidences for the faithful.

Everything is going along well and I feel like a new person. I'm able to personally relate to the term "reborn." It makes sense to me. Then, at some point, usually out of ego or complacency, for me, placing effort slowed down, or ceased completely. I do not recognize it right away because my ego tells me everything is perfect. My ego wants to run the show and opening myself to an outside power cripple it. This is the process where I am moving away from God. The part I want to recognize within this writing is that when I move away, I am left to deal with life, by myself. I no longer have a Captain guiding me. The Spirit wants to be there with me, but I cannot live from ego and with God at the same time. That's defining 'free will' at its core. One of the terms of EGO is Edging God Out. It is never ever the other way around.

What is vitally important for me to remember through it all is He is always there, right in my core, waiting for me. All I have to do is seek. For me seeking comes from silence. Silencing my mouth. Silencing my mind. Silencing all outside noise and opening my heart to feel His presence. The more I 'Feel' the more spiritual connection I have and the less ego I have to deal with.

Lessons Learned in Life: Living in NOW

My readings the past few days have all related to living in the present moment. Over time I have realized that my worries and fears are never tied to the moment I am in, or the place where I stand. They are ALWAYS related to what if, how will I...
Somewhere down the road.

A good example took place in 2007, when I smashed a company car into a tree; I had been drinking. The amount of fear this brought on for me was huge. Fear of going to jail. Fear of losing my job. Fear of not being able to drive because the great state of Michigan would yank my driving privileges. Fear of not having money to pay my obligations. Fear of legal costs and the drama that comes with courts... Endless fears.

Another good example, one, which on several occasions threatened the *no-drinking rule*, I have lived by since soon after the meeting with the tree, was during the child custody to gain 50% time with my son. Every thought I had was fear driven, and although I could not understand it while it was all whirling, every fear was surrounding "out there." I did not think I would ever be able to be his father, or have the opportunity to share the things I felt were important. I thought our life together would consist of every other weekend *drop ins* that I heard so much about, and I hated that thought. The more hatred I felt, the more fearful I became. At one point, my mail would pile up in the mailbox because I was too afraid to find out what might be in there.

I lost the job and license for sixty (60) days, but in return I found a new way to live life. It involved highs such as seeing miracles happening in my life and in the life of others. I was given people to teach me and people I could teach. Because of these events, I know more about unselfish love. I won the 50% custody, which I completely believe is because I did not let the fear of tomorrow determine my actions throughout the process. A small amount of fearlessness and a large amount of God directing the outcome, as always!

I have realized that when I love from the heart, and depend on God, I am immediately guided to correct thinking. God is in the present. He is the Now. This moment. I will never see God's presence in the future. I am only able to see, feel and hear him in the present moment in which I am living. Whenever I am looking into the future, I see myself "out there" alone. I do have all kinds of examples from my past that showed me God will be there with me. This *knowing* from my past, I consider to be faith.

Once I'm ready to stop worrying, the following process, initiated with some deep relaxing breathing helps every time...

1- Stop, take a moment and figure out where you are in your head. I promise it will be future).

2- Bring your thinking into being aware that God is in this moment. Pray that your thinking is in the NOW.

3- Think of your own example of crashes or custody events, when God showed himself in the way events unfolded that were not in your control.

4- Remember who you are. We are all "cups of the ocean" that is God! Sometimes I can do this on my own and a lot of times it helps me to talk to others about where I am. Actually, quite often

I find talking to others about where I am is how I realize I am not living NOW. And if I am really stuck, I find that spending time listening to someone else talk about his or her life, slows my thinking about myself and my troubles.

5- Take whatever next step is in front of you to take.

I hope this helps someone who may have fear ruling his or her thoughts. If you are in that state of mind and you have stumbled onto this reading, I am excited for you! I am excited because it means it is your time to become aware of a life lesson that will awe you!!

Lessons Learned in Life: Student to Life

I do not know anyone who can become a teacher of anything, without first being a student.
Although I am not at the level of my current teachers, my life is more enjoyable, enlightening and peaceful when I'm in the role of the student.

I was living in Wisconsin a few years ago, and at the time I was involved in a fellowship whose mission is based on helping others. I was at a Friday night meeting in downtown Wisconsin with a close friend and mentor of mine. I had been involved in this fellowship for almost a year at the time of this particular meeting. My mentor had been involved for over twenty (20) years at the time.

Inside the meeting room, I sat at a table and my friend sat at another table. I sat at a table with a guy (let's call him Pete). Pete and I connected right away, and we chatted prior to the opening of the meeting. Pete was within his first week of attending meetings, and the more we talked, the more interested he seemed. After the meeting closed, Pete approached me and we talked some more. He seemed very interested in what I had said at the table. Roughly five minutes into talking, my friend joined us, and I introduced him to Pete. They talked for less than one minute (no kidding... one minute) and my friend shook Pete's hand, turned to me and said, 'Let's go." Up to this point, I thought Pete would be an ideal fellow for me to pass on my almost one year of wisdom to, and I was annoyed that my friend so abruptly ended the conversation. 'What the heck, I thought, here is a guy who can use what I have to share with him, and this goofball is ruining my chance." Or 'his' chance, if I'm letting my ego run the show. What a selfish way to be, I thought.

 So, I march out of the meeting and catch up with my friend and ask him, in not so friendly terms, 'What the heck was all that about? I was going to help that guy."

Here's the lesson...

 My friend turned to me and said, "There are two types of people you'll run across. Ones who know what they need to do, when they need to do it and how they need to do it. You cannot do anything for these people. Then there's the person holding out their hands, asking for help. If you're focused on the first person, you are letting people you can really help pass you by."

So as much as I learn and know and experience in my life, I want to continue to carry the number two guy inside me. Being involved in a speaker circuit for change and motivation, I speak about what I know because that's what I have to give. That is one of the reasons this blog is so passionate for me, as it helps me share my life's lessons with the world. But at the same time, listening, reaching out for help and learning are pivotal for my spiritual awakening. As much as I want to affect the universe, I also want to be the guy that listens to new understandings and ask to be shown new ways. I think every great teacher remains a student.

These are my words of encouragement; I am interested in hearing yours! I'd really like to hear back from whomever receives this message. It is great to start such a discussion.

Lessons Learned in Life: Living my Decisions

"I'm willing to go beyond the 50-yard line for people, as long as they are willing to meet me somewhere outside their own goal line."

That is how a friend of mine explains today's lesson... Like most of the people I know, I understand the need to compromise and since its part of my daily responsibility to review my actions on a regular basis, I can honestly say I compromise more that 50% in my relationships very regularly.

Too often in my past I have found myself at other people's five (5)-yard line, I hear them telling me, "Keep coming, you're almost there." This IS NOT anyone's fault. Not theirs, nor mine. It just is, and if I am happy with it and they are happy with it, I guess it's OK. From my personal experience, I see it as co-dependent or filling a need to be a saver. That is how I always ended up feeling about it anyway.

Today, my lesson is about me being OK taking the time I need for me. It snowed here last night and today and I really felt this pull to get into the woods with my new snowshoes. Away from traffic, houses, noise and people. Kind of like my Sunday service. Spending time with the Big Guy!

After this, I spent the evening sitting in my cozy home, with the fire place burning, grateful for my life. It does not snow a lot as often as it seemed to when I was a wee lad, so when it does, I really enjoy getting to view it from my great room window, office window, or even my garage, as I excitedly wait for enough snow to start up the snow blower, without my neighbors thinking I have been drinking...

Bringing this all together, in making these choices for the day I have to decline other choices. Choices that someone else would rather I make. Maybe it is because I am turning forty (49) in a week and have experienced living my life through other people's choices, or maybe it is because of the recent reading I was doing, where it said the biggest regret people have on their deathbed is...

Ready...

THEY LIVED TOO MUCH OF THEIR LIVES
BY OTHER PEOPLE'S DECISIONS.

The further I travel my spiritual path, the more important it is becoming for me to determine how and where I spend my life. What I do and do not do. Where I give my time, and what is important to me. Knowing I want to have healthy relationships in my life, it is equally important that I am loving in my decisions and when I refuse a request that it is not done in an unkind manner.

The other big thing I am learning in carrying out this decision in my life is that not everyone will accept my decisions. I realize some will make a choice to see my decisions as an act against them. What do I do with these situations? I love them just as much as I would if they did accept my choices. Someone who does not accept my decisions affords me the opportunity to practice my issues with people pleasing. Everything I read tells me that I cannot help anyone else unless I can help myself; that I am unable to love another unless I have learned to love me. Making decisions that are in my best interest, that fill my heart, and grow my passions are always decisions best for everyone involved.

Lessons Learned in Life: Outlets

If you do not accept who you truly are, nobody else can fulfill the joy you carry within yourself and the entire world will be short changed

Yesterday marked the start of my forty ninth (49th) year in this body. It also brought me news that my Dad, who is back in Arizona, is going to be sent home from the hospital with hospice care. According to his doctor, if he improves over the next several weeks, the medical team will resume his care, but he is too weak at this point to continue treatment. I am having such a hard time, maybe unwillingness is a better way to define it, I am unwilling to give up hope that he can get better.

Anyway, yesterday was my birthday, and I planned to start the day with a hike, snowshoeing up in Clarkston, MI. Once I got started on the hike, my outlet kicked into place, and I spent an hour video recording the hike to send to my Dad, with the hopes of cheering him.

My Dad has always been a rugged outdoorsman and his favorite television shows usually have something *Survival* in the title. I follow his footsteps with this passion. I am very well known in my family for having an unusual sense of humor.

This did get him laughing. In fact, everyone in my family sent me text messages all night and this morning about how crazy I am and how much they laughed!

The point to my writing is this. If I spent too much time considering what I thought the right thing to do would be, I would not have chosen to share my creativity (even if it is goofy) the way I did. In doing so, my actions have lifted the spirits of my entire family, by giving us seven (7) minutes of something to focus instead of the current situation we, as a family, are facing.

Each of us has talents and gifts that are meant to be shared. Those talents will be called on and we will know when to act on them every time we are supposed to. All we have to do is trust. Trust that we are perfect, whatever talent we have is perfect for the situation, and by using these talents and gifts is how God's strength and almightiness will be revealed.

So again, I say, "If you don't be who you truly are, nobody else can fulfill the joy you carry within yourself and the entire world will be shortcutted." (my blog, my word...lol)

These are my words of wisdom, from my experiences.

Lessons Learned in Life: Own My Creatorship (part A)

I breathed on Friday with my Breath-work Master. And like every time I breathe, new insights come to me. "I OWN MY CREATORSHIP" is the slogan that came out of this session. These words hit me with such power and strength. I felt it vibrate through my entire being, with a knowing or maybe remembering.

A 'lil background, I have been carrying around a hurt within me over a text event that happened almost seven (7) years ago. It is not near as strong a pain as it was, but there are still glimmers of it within me. Back in 2007, during the process of relocating my family from Michigan to Wisconsin, I was driving from Indiana to Wisconsin when I received a text from my now ex-wife stating, "This is awkward, but I filed for divorce today." It hit me hard for many reasons. I was floored that someone could send such a message by text. I felt so much anger about the way this communication was handled.

Right after my breath session on Friday I received a text message from a sister that stated, "The hospital is sending Father home from

46

Hospice because his condition is too bad for them to continue treatment." This hit me the same way as the other text had. Hard! It immediately brought up the same emotions I felt seven years ago. I felt so much anger towards her for sending me such intimate emotional information using a cold text message.

Because of how enlightening the words hit me "I own my creatorship" and this new understanding these words brought to me, I was able to make a conscious decision that I didn't need to re-create a repeat of the emotions from seven years ago.

This is where it gets cool!

IMMEDIATELY after asking myself what do I want to create, I felt relieved of the anger and hurt about not only my sister's text about my Father, but also the text I received seven (7) years ago. It instantly made sense that I focused on the text message because it was so much easier to deal with over the content of the text. It made perfect sense!! As all these awareness's are flowing within me, I could feel my body release the pain, and I could feel it move away from me. I even felt my Soul saying, "Thank you and good bye" as the whole event was taking place.

My words of wisdom are these: take ownership of your creatorship. Make that conscious decision to create your experiences.

Lessons Learned in Life: Owning my Creatorship (Part B)

 Such words of encouragement and what an AWESOME mantra this is turning out to be!

"I Own My Creatorship".

Say it out loud... I OWN MY CREATORSHIP

Say it again and let it sink into your heart. I OWN MY CREATORSHIP...

 For the past five days, these words have brought about a new way of viewing and understanding to my life. Today's lesson came in a "moving mountains" kind of way. It taught me that I do not have to orchestrate the world. I only have to make a decision on what I choose to create and the world will work around my desires.

 Sound like b.s.? I would have thought so too. But what is the likelihood of this example that follows happening at this precise point and time? Owning my creatorship does not mean I push people out... As stated in my previous article, I found out on Friday my Dad was being taken off his doctor's care for his cancer and was being placed in Hospice. Not knowing what to do, I make a seven (7)-minute video clip of myself hiking. It was silly and meant to make Dad laugh. It succeeded. You can read the details and view the video in Owning My Creatorship (Part A).

That's important for this next part to make sense...

During a discussion with a close friend about the video, my friend determined his opinion was required about the video project. His point was how I could have improved my efforts and made the project "better" in his opinion.

My thought in the moment was that I do not want to create someone else critiquing my project. I do not want my feelings, of using a healthy outlet for myself, taken away from me.

Additionally, my "original video" provided my Father the laughter I was hoping it would. This thought led to my initial comment: that the way the project turned out was perfect just as it was. The conversation led to frustration from the other person. Within a very short time, maybe a few minutes at most, the person got up and left my home. I would describe him as being very angry (trust me on this, I've driven enough people to anger to consider myself somewhat of an expert).

After their departure, it HIT me like a ton of bricks...his leaving was because I took ownership over my creatorship. Like I said earlier, I had decided at the start of the conversation that I did not need to experience negative criticism and in doing so, ultimately (but very quickly) the tension created the departure. I did not have to be upset, angered, or explain myself or ask the person to leave. It all unfolded with my feelings of loving myself, and the person I was with. As soon as he left, I was able to feel tremendous gratitude for the video I had created. I enjoyed my creativeness as a perfect work.

And it felt REJUVENATING!

All the reading and listening I've been doing for so long is fitting together now. I don't have to create the specific details. I only have to decide what I want to experience (create). God and the universe will work as one on the details of how it will come to me, but I can be certain it will show up. The clearer I can be about the details of what the experience will look like, the more power I will be putting into the creation.

In my closing words of wisdom, I guess this is what the bible refers to as us all having the power to move mountains. FINALLY, I can stop trying to push them to where I want them!!

Lessons Learned in Life: The passing of my Hero (the unfolding)

Words of Encouragement about a Great Man and a new understanding for me!

Haven't written in a week because I've been spending all my time in a hospice center in Gilbert Arizona, along with as much of my family as physically possible, waiting for my Dad's soul to release his body to an eternity of freedom. To a dimension I do not fully comprehend yet. We spend our days, and some of us nights, talking to him, counting the time between his breaths hoping everything we believe is true about the after death. We cry and pray, both individually and together. We spend time talking to Dad, again individually as well as a group as well.

Although I do believe this to be a blessing to be here with Dad, my thinking gets a bit confused and asks me why we are all sitting here waiting for this wonderful man to pass. I'm not ashamed that it takes talking to my teachers to realize that we are waiting to celebrate the place he is going. A place I choose to believe is to be awed.

I have had this idea of taking some time through all this and driving to Sedona. It started with my son and I getting away for a few hours. I thought this was the purpose for the journey. So that he and I would have some time together. His unwillingness to do so reminded me that my decision for him and I to spend time together to make this drive was one sided. It fulfilled what I thought we need, but it did not take into account what is best for him or his needs. I have not made the trip because I did know if I am supposed to. Then today, during a conversation with my favorite master teacher, I realized the purpose of the trip is to do so with my Dad.

This thought sounds a bit confusing for me, even as I write it. My head is telling me that I should be here at the hospice center to share in the moment of my Dad's passing, along with everyone else. Not only to console my family but also to stand side-by-side with whomever is present for the final good bye to Dad's human form.

My heart, now that is a different message all together. My heart is giving me feelings that say to have a great adventure with Dad prior to his soul passing to higher dimensions. It's telling me to get in the car, pick up coffee and orange slices (his favorite snack, only second to Nutty Bars) and head out to Sedona. Let our souls visit Devils Bridge and sit there and enjoy the awesomeness of whatever we see together.

In seeing this whole vision from this view, it makes sense that this being a time of celebration. Up until now, my Dad has not been able to be directly involved in my hiking/backpacking trips until I return and discuss them with him.

I believe this trip to Sedona to be a door opener to the realization that Dad will be right there alongside me throughout the whole adventure. And if I am correct about that (which I am pretty sure I am), then the door is wide open for him to be right there with me and all of us through eternity.

I am not sure if these could be considered words of wisdom, but it is my awakening!!

Lessons Learned in Life: Our drive to Sedona together

I preference this writing with stating that I am still are still having a tough time accepting the following accounts. I have explained the accounts to my mentors, and they all tell me the same thing. I can choose to believe everything that happened during this trip, or I can choose not to. Either way is correct.

I never liked answers like that!

This is a continuation of my previous writing. When I figured out the trip, I was supposed to make to Sedona was not with my son. It was with my dying father who laid in a bed at a wonderfully caring hospice center in Gilbert Arizona...

Even after my last writing I sat in the hospice center trying to remove the thoughts and feelings about making this trip. Basically, because I wanted to be there for my family. Somewhere between 2:00 & 2:30, the feelings became strong enough that I told my sister that I was leaving. I told her a bit of the inner direction I was feeling, so she was not surprised when I finally made the decision.

In fact, she stated that my decision took long enough. I left the hospice center and filled the fuel tank. I also bought a bottle of water and a bag of orange slices. These were Dad's favorite road snack. I plugged Sedona into my GPS and off I went.

From early on in the trip, I tried to make connection with my Dad. I did so through my thoughts, trying mental telepathy. I do not really even understand what that is, but I figured it was worth a try. I tried feeling his presence from my heart... nothing. Then I tried actually talking to him, as if he were sitting in the passenger seat... nothing. I didn't get it, but somehow, I knew I was doing exactly what I was supposed to be doing with this whole trip. I somehow knew I was helping him to leave his human body through this act.

Somewhere between an hour and an hour and a half outside Sedona I felt my dad's presence. He did not arrive in a shocking way or anything like that. It was calm. It was untouchable but without question, he was there with me. There were no words at first, just a feeling of his presence. I don't know when the conversation started and I do not know how much was verbal, how much thought or how much feeling, but I recollect all three forms were involved. I do not remember what exactly he said at first because I was so awed at this unfolding right before me. Maybe something about my driving because I remember stating, 'That's not funny" then a minute later "Well, maybe a little' and I smiled and I know he did too, although I did not see his face.

Again, as I'm writing this, I'm trying to be as detailed as I can, but I really have no idea if my communications were thoughts, feelings or verbal.

At one point I asked Dad, if he can describe for me where he was and what it looked like. His only word was 'nope.' I waited some time to see if he would elaborate, but he didn't. Once I realized what I was waiting for I laughed because this was exactly his nature. I remember having a sense that he was comfortable and secure. Calm and at ease with where he was.

There was a lot of quiet time in between our communications, like when the two of us took long drives and neither of us felt like we had to talk the whole time. I knew he was there though.

And he knew I knew. At one point I remember thinking to myself, maybe I should ask him if there is anything, I should pass on for him. The moment I did this, a picture of my mom popped up in the front of my head (almost like I could see her in the windshield) and the response I received was, "Thank her for an incredible love and an incredible life." Sometime latter a vision of my older brother popped up, exactly as my mom had. The response I received was number one. Somehow, I knew it didn't mean oldest and within moments I realized it meant the torch has been officially passed within our family. The other thing I knew from the response is that I was supposed to support my brother and assist him however I could. Sometime later my sister popped up. The older of the two and the response was, "I adore her."

Sometime passed without any communications, but again, I knew he was there. Almost like he was enjoying the scenery of the mountains. After a while I tried to put a picture of me in the place, I had seen my other family members. I tried this a few times until I finally received the response 'you already know.'

By this time, we rolled into Sedona and I

expected we were going to head up to Devils Bridge, thinking we would be getting out of the car and walk a bit and enjoy the scenery. Like most times when I try to implement my will when I should be following, we pulled and I recognized this feeling that had been with me since we reached the towns edge. It was direction to turn around and head back. I drove almost three (3) hours without ever getting out of the car and drive back. I thought. My next thought was, 'I don't mind giving you a ride but you could have given me gas money.' I laughed and I am not sure if I heard his laughter, but I knew he laughed too.

 As I headed back it seemed like his presence faded. I felt like he was still with me but it felt like a lessor portion than on the way into town. A bit into the trip back I picked up my phone, which I had not done all the way to Sedona. There were two voice mails on my phone. One from my younger brother and one from the oldest sister. I called my brother and he answered. I knew why they were calling. He asked where I was and a few other questions. I finally said, "Dad died, didn't he?" He responded, "Yes." I asked if he was O.K. and got off the phone. Next, I contacted my sister and when she answered she immediately said, "You were right Joey, Dad was waiting for you to take him on you the trip." We both started crying and I told her what he said about her; that he adored her. We cried more.

I little later my son called me and asked where I was. Without explaining I told him I was about an hour and a half away (which was an underestimate) and he told me my mom was going to be angry if I was not there in a hurry. I called my sister back and asked to talk to mom without explaining all the details. She did, and I was able to talk to my mom, who asked me, "Did you have to go so far?" I told her what my Dad said about her. We also cried together on the phone. She explained she had given everyone direct instructions that nothing was to happen until I arrived back at the hospice center; I so much appreciated her doing so. The rest of the trip back I spent trying to sort through everything that had happened; I was trying to make sense of it all.

Although in the past I have not given much credit to souls communicating, I am sold on the idea from this point forward. It starts with a belief in its being a possibility. From there I must say, since I have started working on learning to feel direction from my soul, instead of thinking my way through life, my life is on an entirely different path. I stated in my Dad's eulogy, now instead of recording my hiking trips and sharing them with him after the fact, he can be right there with me as it all unfolds.

My Dad always seemed to have words of wisdom for us during difficult times. Like now, I expect he is saying, I'm still here to lean on and receive guidance from. Just ask and believe the answer will come!

Lessons Learned in Life:

Today I learned that I am not my experiences or my emotions or my thoughts.

Today I learned that I have wasted so much time out of my life manipulating others to be who I wanted them to be, and now it's MY TIME to find my self-awareness.

Today, I learned that life is enjoyable, even when I have emotions about things.

Today I know love differently than I ever have before.

My questions... Who am I?

My affirmation... Everything is perfect in my life and my cup overflows with overwhelming abundance!

Lessons Learned in life: Patience

Today I learned that when I start rushing or pushing to make things happen, it is typically because I am afraid that whatever it is, I am trying to force into manifestation will fade and not come to fruition, if I do not make it come true.

At these times, it is so refreshing to remember that I do not need to push, pull, and battle to make events happen. To be reminded over and over that the desires of my heart will find me. All I have to do is believe they will arrive exactly when they are supposed to.

What an awesome way to go through life, compared to pushing to make thing happen. I am grateful!

My Question: What is it I really want to happen? How much time do I allow my imagination to bring detail to my desires?

My Affirmation: Everything I desire always shows up for me at the Perfect time, in an amazing way, and all I have to do is be me!

Lessons Learned in Life... Own my thoughts

Today I learned again that I get to determine what emotions I will feel and which ones I can discard. I woke up this morning and it was the first day I didn't have immediate thoughts of sadness over my Dad passing away.

As soon as I recognized that I felt guilty. Something within me felt like I should feel bad the entire day, with thoughts of "how much did you actually love him, Joe". The initial condemning and defensive thoughts came up within me. As if I were arguing with someone who was falsely accusing me of something, but both the condemnation and the defensiveness were coming from the same source... ME.

After taking a few minutes to stop and make sense of what was unfolding (all in my head, mind you), I realized it was some old programming that no longer served me or anyone else. I purposely put thoughts into my mind (in an affirmation sort of way) that reminded me of how much I loved my Dad and instead of feeling overwhelming sadness my thoughts are healthy.

My Question: Are there other arguments going on within me of which I am unaware?

My Affirmation: I only hold onto thoughts that serve me, and I determine on what my mind focuses.

Lessons Learned in Life: Inactivity is more productive

Today I learned that it is more difficult to stop activity and trust the workings of my imagination to find me. That I have programming within me that tells me I have to give 120% in order to receive the desires of my heart.

All my teachings give opposition to this philosophy. They tell me to use my imagination to create a clear vision and then all I have to do is wait expectantly. Since everything I've learned to date, has shown me that by being is where I've found God, my true self, peace and solitude, I have to believe it is correct in this situation as well.

I am currently putting this to test, which brings up my learning for today. I have a very detailed view of the life I want. I allow my imagination time on a daily basis to further develop my view.

Today I noticed during my free-flowing imagination time that inside I really wanted to develop the plan (the how to). I spent time going to several stores seeking material that would assist in laying out the path. Then later this evening, during my reading time, the message came to me about the importance of being in place of doing. I was instantly grateful I wasn't able to find the material I went hunting for.

My Question: Can it be that the only thing that's held me up from having the life of my dreams is my trying to do it, rather than being and letting it come to me?

My Affirmation: I create what I imagine. The plan/path is none of my business. All I have to focus on is using my imagination to develop the view of my dream, then trust that it will come.

Lessons Learned in Life: Grief

Today I learned that sadness is as much a part of life as is overwhelming happiness and if I don't let it flow through me, I cannot be whole. I also learned the gratitude of having someone close with whom to share my grief.

Today was a tough day. It started upon waking up with thoughts of Dad. I awoke with a complete lack of any ambition or motivation, to the point of having to push myself to take a shower and get busy with my job. Soon into the morning I received a phone call from my sister. I could tell right away that we shared the same mood.

Almost as soon as we started talking, she began crying and talking about how difficult it is dealing with losing our Father; although I did not know I needed it, she ultimately gave me permission to feel my emotions. I believe I would not have let those emotions process through me today, had I not have talked to her. She is my angel!!

We were able to alter the conversation to talk about where Dad is and how feeling his presence only requires me to be calm and quiet. That I do not have to go out seeking him. That I only have to be calm and be aware for his presence.

My Question: will this overwhelming feeling of loss ever calm for more than a few minutes?

My Affirmation: I know you're in a place to be awed and your spirit is right beside me, at all times! I love you Dad,

Lessons Learned in Life: Creatorship is under way

 Today I learned that my Creatorship is growing at a rapid rate. I am taking more and more responsibility for all the areas of my life. The parts that could be judged awesome, as well as those not so desirable areas.

 I do not know about anyone else, but If through God, I have ultimate control of my life, then I want to ensure I am creating with purpose.
Anything I choose to ignore within myself creates, at a subconscious level, causes two important pitfalls.

1) The subconscious creates at a more rapid rate and with increased depth.

2) When the subconscious is focusing on something undesirable for my life, it is not able to work on the miracles I choose to come to fruition.

 With that being said, whenever I have fear, worry or sadness in my body, it automatically creates at a higher level than what I consciously create.

Not only am I somehow able to spend more time imagining with more specific detail than I've ever been able to before, but I am also finding cheerleaders showing up for me in all areas of my life. People who are supporting me with so many kind, loving and uplifting words. I am grateful to their willingness to support my dreams with financial backing.

 My Question: Am I choosing to identify giving up my crutches to have the life I desire? The life I dream of?

 My Affirmation: I feel every feeling that shows up for me, without judgement and without crutches!

Lessons Learned in Life: Gratitude

Today I learned something pretty big. I learned that happiness is in this moment and is not someplace to get to or grow into. I learned that I can be happy right here and now, and it is only a decision I make. It is also not contingent on anything or anyone else. It really is an inside job. I thought I had to be alone for a certain amount of time, and happiness would come to me. It is not like that however, happiness starts the moment I decide to be!!

Today I learned that struggling is not how to advance. The best things in my life came to me at times when I was content taking care of what was in front of me. Today I realized a little more that I have a God given power within me to create the life I choose, to have health, prosperity and happiness. Today I learned for some reason, that I made a decision in my life that living in "lack" is how I was supposed to live. I also learned I want to make a different choice from this moment forward.

My questions for today are: Can I focus enough on my feelings and actions to create the life I want?

My affirmation for today is... Thank you God! My thinking and your blessings combined are creating a most beautiful and fruitful life that I get to share with others. I am perfect & always open to receiving God's best!!

Lessons Learned in Life: I Am

Today I learned that the positive quotes my Spiritual Mentors make have taken on a whole new concept for me. I have been mimicking their words without realizing the full impact until today. Quotes such as, 'You are absolutely perfect exactly as you are'.

Up until this point I understood and utilized these words as my defense mechanism against someone's attacks, criticisms or anyone's need to be critical towards me. I did not use them in a "gotcha" manner, or payback sort of way, but as a means of building my healthy self-esteem. And guess what? These phrases have brought astonishing changes to my life. Better results than anything I have tried to this point. Using these phrases internally, as well as externally to the folks I needed to stand up against have helped me to halt allowing my life to be led based on others' words, thoughts and desires.

Learning these words of wisdom have been an insightful experience for a guy like me. And in addition, tonight I was given the gift of a whole new level of understanding and appreciation for these motivational phrases!

Are ya'll ready for this?? Lol

 I realized that by allowing these I words to penetrate my soul; I do not have a need for a defense. Let me say it a different way. By believing the truth, "that we are all perfect reflections of God" I have no need for a defense... Make sense? Let me explain further. When I know without a doubt who I am, it does not make any difference to me what someone says or does to me. It cannot rock me. If I know me as God knows me, somebody's criticism of me will not be able to alter one sliver of my being.

 In reverse, when I was half-believing in my being a miracle, anytime someone critiqued me, in any way, their words became my battle field for self-sabotage and self-doubt. The less we know who we are, the more likely someone can convince us of who they need or see us to be. Someone very dear to me once told me, "Unless you fully know yourself, at some point someone will come along and sell you a bill of goods that will do irreparable damage to your self-esteem." I now realize the truth of these words. I also realize that it does not say if I know myself, or partially know myself. It says, I have to "fully know myself."

I'm not saying it does not take practice to stop my thinking, open my soul, and let these words permeate my being, because it does, but what a rewarding declaration!!

So yet again, through owning my Creatorship, I am reaping benefits so wide and so far beyond what I could have ever imagined, and the awesome thing about it is that it all proves... We are all huge rock stars... Diamonds, not in the making, but brilliantly dazzling rocks, and all we have to do is admit to it and see ourselves as wonderful essences of God, and we will shine for the world to see and from which to grow!

Lessons Learned in Life – Beliefs

Today I learned that God's only experience is love... he has no power to hurt or harm...

God cannot not love...

In addition, I learned that seeking God has nothing to do with spending time in my beliefs... To truly seek God, I need to be willing to look outside what I already believe God to be.

My affirmation... I am so much loved by God!

Lessons Learned in Life: Acceptance

Today I learned ACCEPTANCE. Again! For some reason I have had this belief that with acceptance comes happiness, when what really happens is by allowing acceptance, I can turn my focus to the things that make me happy...

The death of my Dad seems like the hardest thing I've faced in my life, thus far. By applying my initial beliefs of acceptance to this situation would mean that I become happy about his death. Sounds ridiculous, right? But how many things do I apply this way of thinking? In my past I would have told myself things like, "He's in a better place" or "I'm grateful for the time I had with him." These are all true statements of acceptance, but as the final result, not the initiation stage.

Another example is when my son told me he was going to live at his Mom's house full time when he turned eighteen (18), which is happening this April. Utilizing the belief that acceptance equals happiness would mean I would feel upbeat and excited about his decision, which was quite the opposite of my initial internal reaction.

Both of these situations brought intense, very

unhappy pain. And this is where the twist comes in.

For me, acceptance is not a decision so much as a path. ..A sizable chunk of that path is allowing the sadness, frustration, anger....Whatever emotions appear. Allowing the pain is where healthy acceptance applies.

With regards to my son, once I allowed the pain of hearing his decision to impact me, which took the better part of three days, and it still sneaks up on me like the hiccups as we approach April, I am able to remember my feelings of respect for him for talking to me man-to-man about the subject. I am able to be proud of myself for being the parent I have been. I'm able to remember I didn't move back from Wisconsin to obtain 50% custody for his benefit as much as I did for mine because I couldn't imagine not being involved in his growing up. But none of these positive events truly come to fruition until I first acccpt whatever emotion it initially caused in me. I can fake like the good thoughts and feeling are there, but everything is masked by the un-dealt with emotions, so nothing will feel real. That's because it isn't!

I've spent so much time trying to skip the allowance (acceptance) of emotions to flow through me and jump right into acting as if. Acting as if everything is as I would choose it. Acting as if I'm great with everything. Acting as if nothing bothers me. I've acted as if, right into a recovery program, and thank God I did!

Now with regards to Dad, I have not faced anything similar to this...even though acceptance starts with me allowing myself to feel the pain of the *nevers,* never seeing his physical body as I knew him. Never being able to call him on the phone. Never putting together, a silly video to make him laugh. And so on...), it isn't something that will be better someday. I am realizing the more I accept sadness as being my overall state of mind, the more I see the good in life. I'm starting to really feel that he is in a place to be envied, that I am so very grateful and honored to be able to call him my Father, and I can still talk to him and he will respond to me.

This situation seems so much different than any others I've faced because it doesn't carry that doom and gloom feeling. I feel sad. Sometimes very sad. By allowing myself this emotion of sadness I don't feel negative towards life. In fact, I feel very blessed and grateful for my life, my family & friends, my work, the passions of mine that are coming to life, along with all the love and support I am receiving. Heck, I'm even grateful for jerk-boy! (lol, always grateful for him!!). I've never felt sadness and gratitude at the same time before.

I know that regardless of the situations I face in life if, first and foremost, I accept whatever I am feeling as being exactly perfect; acceptance is well on its way.

Lessons learned in Life: Sharing

Today I learned that I love sharing my Creatorship. Probably as much as any other area of my life. I feel so elated when I get an opportunity to discuss my journey and my experiences and the lessons, I've learned from them.

I feel so thankful to God for my life and the people in my front row!

My affirmation: My cup overflows with gratitude!

Lessons Learned in Life: Forgiveness (the unfolding)

Today I learned that owning my Creatorship means I have to take responsibility for the love as well as any hatred or resentments in my life. Not such an easy pill to swallow!

In trying to understand what true forgiveness is, I realize I do not yet know. It appears I'm in the same position with regards to unconditional love. This was brought to my attention through my great teacher and friend on Friday afternoon, during my breathing session, when she explained to me how my emotions about a matter showed her I held resentment and asked how I would be able to assist anyone else in owning their Creatorship when I'm not owning my own. I so love her!!

In reviewing and writing about love and forgiveness, I found that I know how to keep resentments and dislikes of people, places and things at bay so they don't cause me daily pain like they used to. I know how to adjust my focus and thinking away from areas that still have my emotions tied to them. But if I am going to 'own my Creatorship' and live to my souls highest level, I cannot afford hatred, dislike and discord flowing through me.

There are areas of my life that I say I no longer hold hatred towards, but the instant a situation comes up that involves that person, place or thing referred to above, I get a surge of emotions that run through my veins. Usually the emotion is not happiness. It's more like anger, rage. This shows me I haven't forgiven; I haven't reached unconditional love.

The positive in all this for me is that I know, without a doubt that I will understand and live through unconditional love... That I will know the heart and soul of forgiveness. I am as confident as I am about this because my soul has the desire to know these things and I've never felt a desire of my soul that hasn't been fulfilled. It's like that for all of us.

In addition, just like every other life lesson I've been gifted with, everywhere I turn, new insights and information to assist me show up. Without me seeking it out. As a quick example, I was talking to my Sister today and without her knowing about any of this, she talked to me about forgiveness and how she has learned to employ forgiveness in her life. AWESOME!!! I expect this journey into forgiveness and unconditional love will be filling my writing pages over the next bit of time and I am as excited about sharing this life's lessons as it unfolds within me as I am to hear from you. Your experiences about forgiveness & unconditional love as application to questions, to sticking points and road blocks.

My hope is to spread this area of my life to anyone & everyone who may understand and need and appreciate the commonality of growing spirituality through life's-lessons!

The love & support I am receiving from ya'll humbles me with deep gratitude!!

Lessons Learned in Life: Forgiveness (Part 2)

Today I'm continuing to learn about forgiveness... All day it felt like my soul was jumping for joy, saying to me, "Thank you for honoring me by being willing to seek and grow in this crucial area of my unfolding".

Webster's Dictionary states the following about the word forgive: "To grant pardon for or remission of. To remit. To grant pardon to. To cease to feel resentment against, to forgive one's enemies."

After writing last night I fell into a deep sleep, which is typical after opening and emptying my soul on paper to what it has to say. I woke up in the morning full of questions. Questions like: "If I own my creatorship, which I understand is taking 100% responsibility for every aspect of my life, then where does forgiveness fit into the equation?"

I thought of an example where something of a sizable nature was taken from me. It caused me a lot of pain and anger. I've been carrying this resentment of this for a long time. There has been a lot of growth in regards to this matter. I've experienced emotions which have ranged from raging hatred to unsettled emotions, which I thought was forgiveness. If I choose to look at the matter in the view having to allow forgiveness in order to move on, isn't that the same thing as playing the victim role? Isn't that the same mentality as saying, "Someone did something to me that I didn't want them to do?" Or, it's like saying, " People outside me have control over me, and the events of my life that involve me?" Right now, it seems that any type of forgiveness is tied to being a victim. Another question I can't seem to answer is, wouldn't owning my creatorship show me that I manifested or created the situation in order for me to reveal to myself some aspect of who I really am?" My God Self.

 It seems to me that choosing the victim role would ultimately be my choice to NOT see who I am . The choice to be a victim will continue to bring about events that I label as painful, until I ask myself, "Why am I experiencing this over and over agaln in my life? What is this showing me about myself?" The only benefit I receive from being a victim is the pain to motivate me to develop. In other words, the only benefit in being a victim is it causes me enough discomfort to build the necessary drive within me to know myself better.

The Bible states, "God helps those who help themselves." These words fit perfectly into my interpretation. If I'm a victim, there aren't any actions I can take against outside attacks. BUT if I own my life and everything in it, I can see how my toughest times are necessary and by applying the new knowledge into my life is lifted to a higher plateau. I think this is what Panache means when he states, "We are perfect exactly as we are."

Now for the other side, what I believe to be my revelation. Owning my creatorship means that every event, every situation and every relationship I have ever been involved with was manifested by me. If this is the case, forgiveness would not fit into the situation. It would not have a place in anything I've been through because it was never something "someone did to me." It was all me all along. Even as I re-read this, I have an internal battle going on between what my mind is telling me, vs what my heart/soul is feeling.

My head is telling me "BULL-SHIT. I've been hurt and I get to own this pain! I have full rights to it forever and no one can take that away from me. I've been hurt and I will make damn sure it never happens again! By ANYONE!" My soul, on the other hand, is clapping and saying, "I've made it! I've arrived on the next floor of my awakening. I now know I can trust myself fully so I no longer have a need to repeat lessons." What a peaceful, exhilarating feeling!!

Lessons Learned in Life: Creatorship awakened

Today I am seeing the benefits of owning my Creatorship! Again today, I felt like although I was part of the world around me, it was from a different angle, or level. Situations that arose had only moments of my emotions and I automatically recognize their value to me and felt a sense of gratitude.

I had several situations occur throughout the day today. I won't go into specific details, due to anonymity, but I will say that all three of the situations that stand out would typically pull on my emotions. The first would pull anger, the second would be resentments no the third would hit me in the sadness department. Not too long ago, I would have spent the day fighting negative feelings. My ego would have started issuing orders about who was wrong, who was right and now to put each situation in order. Or I would have gone in the other direction and withdrew from everyone involved. Kind of waited for the wind to die down; I did neither.

Instead I breathed when I felt emotions rising. Only a handful of breathes is all it took for me to see that my real desire was to be of assistance in all three situations.

It was right there, in the frontal lobe of my mind. I knew as the situations were unfolding that my only will was to be of help. That allowed me to sidestep all the ego stuff and focus on what was being told to me. With that information I was able to ask questions. The only real purpose of my questions was to help the person I was speaking to see the whole thing in a light of their favor of choices.

I feel so humbled in my life. In these works that I GET to do. How awesome is this!

My questions: My big question right now is how can I expand my works to reach a minimum of one million people within 2014?

My affirmation: The person who is awakening I can assist will seek and find me!

Lessons Learned in Life: Day of Gratitude

Today I felt my ownership of my Creatorship, in a very big way! I'm not going to spoil the surprise, but I am so excited about what is about to unfold! And the awesome part is that I get to share it with all of you...

Can't say anything more, for the moment, even though I'm a bit nervous I've developed a twitch trying to keep it a secret... Lol

Over the past several months so many of my desires are unfolding and with such little effort on my part. There are angels showing up throughout my life encouraging, supporting and loving me. On top of that, I am hearing people I've known my whole life making statements about me that floor me. I feel this incredible increase in my desire to share everything I've been taught.

I laugh at this thought, "How is it a goofball like me, the same guy who filmed a silly video to make Dad laugh, able to have all the miracles unfold that I'm experiencing?" The bigger question is if it can happen for me, can it surely happen in your life as well?

I say Absolutely!

My Questions: How awesome is it to be a part of this shift and who can I share it with for both our betterment?

My Affirmation: Through it all, I will be me, and that will be precisely what is required!

Lessons Learned in Life: The Easy Decisions

Today I'm receiving more depth in my understanding about forgiveness and even getting a hunch into unconditional love. In looking at forgiveness through my sight of 'Owning My Creatorship', the understanding of "why things are happening in my life" are showing up so much quicker than they ever have. And they are showing up with a knowing, compared to a sort of guessing. It isn't a constant stream of excitement either. Sometimes it's accompanied with emotions of sadness and loss and hurt and fear riding shotgun.

Thank God today I have tools to help me separate the emotions from the truths. Tools to help me process the emotions without having to sacrifice the lesson. It is a blessing to see which way to navigate at a fork in my path. It's a double blessing to be able to stay on that path when it gets rough and emotions start trying to take over as pilot-in-command. I, like probably many of us, have spent a lot of time in my life making decisions out of it being easier, or less fearful over making the decision I knew to be the right one.

This next paragraph or so shows great testimony to my recent articles regarding forgiveness. For prior to my new understanding of "forgiveness is allowing the victim in" I would not have been able to think, discuss or write about what I'm about the write about without anger being at the forefront of my mind. Anger strong enough to block my heart and soul!

Anyway, when I look at some highlights from my past, I stayed in a marriage for almost twenty (20) years that had no business existing beyond the three-year mark. There was a love of some sorts, the best we each knew love to be at the time, and the most precious trusted gift God could put in a man's life. My son!

During this marriage there was a lot of hurt inflicted, I'm sure from both sides, although my focus has always been on the receiving end. There were several times we met crossroads, facing the decision to go on separate and although I knew that would be best, it was so much easier to make the decision I/we made. There were things that happened that I won't spend the words to mention specifics about. There was a separation at year 4 or 5, semi divorce proceedings not quite to completion and finally, a one-year divorce 2.5 years after the first attempt. By this time, we were approaching the 20th year anniversary. There was a nine-year-old boy who shut himself down to deal with the process. It was indescribably ugly. It was immensely fearful. It was completely heartbreaking...

 I went through all of this, including allowing a nine-year-old boy to be affected because I wanted the easier decision. I drank myself into a DUI to deal with not wanting to make the harder decision. I said things to a human being that I now pray God had his ears covered because I wanted to make the easier decision. Do you see what I'm getting at? I ask you, the reader as well as my soul is asking me!

 Based on my beliefs at the time about marriage & divorce, based on my inability to love myself, based on the amount of self-abuse I learned to absorb in order to keep things from changing, I would not, or could not have taken the tough steps towards the best decision. I had to choose the easier one. I chuckle as I'm writing this because I'm wondering if as a reader you're thinking, "Are you mad? How could staying in something so dark & ugly be the easier decision?"

OR...

 Maybe you're like me. Maybe you can scan back over your life and remember that BIG event where you brought so much hell onto yourself because you thought the other decisions that laid in front of you were more difficult to make, and keep! A time where you clearly came to rest at a crossroad. Clearly saw your available paths. Thought of each one independently from the other. Felt a sense of which one you were supposed to take... And then... made a conscious choice to go with the one that seemed easier, less emotional, less fearful, for that moment, turned the wheel in that direction and stepped on the accelerator to move forward. If you are like me, it turned into one of the most emotional roller coaster rides of your life!

 The good news is that we are all supposed to go through these events in order to be who we are today. In fact, if you've been keeping up on my posts, you know that I believe we create these events in our lives in order to teach us who we are. We orchestrated every detail so we could go forward with more wisdom about ourselves. It is our growth mechanism bringing into our lives what we manifest so that we can grow, flourish

and become one with our soul! The other people involved are only brining the message we are asking to be brought.

As I walk forward on understanding forgiveness, unconditional love, my decision-making process and my decision sticking process, I feel grateful for my previous wife ability to make the tough decision. To stick to and see that decision through that freed us as prisoners and has opened this awesome, amazing life I now get to be passionate about, write about, share and learn more about!!

I hope the person who needs to hear these words receives them. If you have, please let me know at **lifes.lessons48@gmail.com.** Completely confidential!

And for all my other readers, I love you and thank you for helping that person who needs the things I write about find them by spreading the word about lifes-lessons.com!!

Lessons Learned in Life... Eagle Spirit

Today, I heard it... I heard it loud and clear! It's really the first time I've heard it in quite some time. Although it came from outside myself, the moment the words were spoken something inside me said, "It's about time, this has been going on long enough and needs to stop." Oh, that's not all it said...lol it continued, "Now we can get back to the life we know."

Owning Our Creatorship...

The words were simply, "We got to pay the bills." Seems harmless, right? A couple years back I would have signed up to that same way of thinking. Today, I felt the potential harm these words can cause and I know that feeling so very well, because I lived with it most of my life.

The conversation was surrounding me talking about how much passion I have for this "Owning My/Your Creatorship" and recently my regular job seems like work. It hasn't been that way, with regards to my current employment situation. It's been six years of feeling excited about finding leads and cold calling. Making that first appointment and steering that initial meeting into something I could sink my teeth into. A quote. It's been the charge of having say-so into the final pricing and negotiating final terms. The sense of achievement of being awarded the purchase orders. It's been tenacity flowing through me. My job has allowed me to deliver on my favorite quote, 'failure is not an option.'

 Right now, the above paragraph best describes how I feel about my passion to help people open their souls, find their paths and live in awesome peace, manifesting their soul's desires and spreading the awakening world-wide! I am finding as my passion in this work gains momentum, my work is temporarily seeming more like work. A job. Tasks... Am I being clear...lol Ok, so going back to the 'words' that I heard so clearly today. Why wouldn't these words try to guide me back to familiar ground, I did my 1st freakin' live radio interview! HELLO!! My blog is spreading like wildfire!! People are showing up and it seems in them doing their work supports and assists me in doing mine!!!!

I realize there are still beliefs within me from past programming... Beliefs like, "You have to have a typical job or quit pipe dreaming." Which I found out later in life is NOT dreaming with a lit pipe. "You are not that important, keep your day job, and quit living in fantasy land." I think you get the point, although there are more thoughts trying to grab hold of me. Trying to convince me that this is a passing phase that will be a waste of time.

STOP...

That was my word of reply to myself. Delivered in a 'cap lock' sort of way.

I did that because it helps me to allow myself a break from my thinking long enough to focus on my breathing. Focusing on my breathing allows me to get in touch with my spirit.

My eagle spirit reminds me that there are no boundaries, no limits, no roadmap, no can't nots (did not know how to write that one). There are beliefs, but ultimately, they are determined by me, by my Creatorship, for my life. The fear I feel comes about from any feelings of unworthiness whirling around inside me. It's fear of all these amazing people and events that support me and my passions not being real, which I thought I settled when I chose to believe the drive I took to a Sedona on January 23rd was with my a Dad and the moment I felt his presence in the car was the same time he left his human body.

Those thoughts that grab hold from words of lack, of not being good enough, or not measuring up, or not deserving may show up from time to time in my life, as well as they may for you, the reader. What I am noticing is life seems to be bringing me much bigger opportunities in between the hiccups of old programming. How awesome is that?! How awesome is it that even after the negative emotions are thanked and passed, I find myself with added blessings, on a higher level of gratitude and the whole process deepens my knowing and awakening!

AWESOME!

Lessons Learned in Life... Living in Excitement

Today I learned that no matter where I go, I will find people who are willing and people who are unwilling to talk to me about 'Owning Our Creatorship'... In fact, there are people out there that are unwilling to talk to me at all... True dat.

I landed in Las Vegas tonight. I am here for a business conference. I don't drink and I am spending the financial gifts bestowed upon me in a responsible manner, so I've decided not to gamble. So, what's left for a guy like me to do...

Survivor Dude walks again!!

Dropped into the center of the most active town in the US, with nothing but my luggage (large suitcase with enough clothes to last a month, plus a fully loaded back pack), my camera, two extra batteries, all the charging chords, a nifty belt holster and a WILL to find out what people think of when they hear the words "Own Your Creatorship."

That's right folks, Survivor Dude does Vegas. Except this time, "what happens in Vegas is hopefully spread around the freakin world!!

That was fun! For those who know me, know about Survivor Dude (my You Tube almost series).

I've started my documentary about "Owning Our Creatorship" and I thought, what better place to start gathering information than the last place on earth a sensible person would go. Right? Right?? And what better time to do so than when there are hundreds of thousands of people gathered for a construction conference. Ok, as I write this, I'm realizing maybe not my best plan, but there have been much, much worse! Anyways, I've started collecting my information and surprisingly enough found a handful of people that were willing to talk to me on tape. I also found someone who would talk but didn't feel comfortable being taped. I even had the opportunity to talk with a person who, immediately after my introduction of my mission said... And I quote, 'it means nothing and we have to go'.

There will be more to come on my research. But following is what I learned from this experience today...

This life is such an awesome ride!! I love it!! And I was reminded today, at precisely the exact moment I needed to hear it that "we don't have to go out there or do something to realize how awesome life is. We only have to recognize it and be open for it to flow to us!!

 Amazingly blessed whether we choose to see it or not!!

Lessons Learned in life: Crabby in Vegas

Today I learned that a larger portion of my worth is tied to my actions than I realized up to this point. This came clear as I looked back at my business travel last week to Las Vegas. I attended a three-day conference in Vegas. Las Vegas has the absolute largest convention center I've experienced. Roughly nine miles a day walking through the show. Huge!

In my normal mode of operation, as I state proudly that I spend the company's money as if it were mine, I stayed at the low-end hotel. In fear of getting into legal trouble I will not mention the name of the establishment, but if you're interested, contact me and I'll gladly prevent anyone from following the same path.

During this three-day event I noticed what I can only describe as being crabby and irritable. Two feelings I hardly ever experience anymore. It grew until I left and started the drive to Arizona, where I was heading to spend the weekend with my Mom. I spent some time during my drive trying to figure out why I felt the way I did during the conference.

I got nothing...

Until I was starting to fill out my expense report today. It hit me...
WHAMMMMMMM!!

The reason I felt like I did in Vegas was because instead of allowing my-self a good clean restful environment after long days, I allowed myself to buy into the belief of cheaper being better. Although I wasn't aware of what this decision was saying to me about me, I made decisions based on the belief that I didn't deserve a more expensive room ($40 more per night to be precise) and I allowed that belief to lock in even deeper, based on my false ego that I was doing it for my company...

How funny is that? I don't get rest in order to save $40/night, so I'm not as productive as I could be, all under the premise that I'm benefiting the company.

"I am worth only what I believe I am worth." I've read this so many times, in so many different books and writings, yet I put myself in rundown, beat up, loud, stinky accommodations, when I should be seeking out the best place for the situation, I am in. It's another example of me taking a belief that is beneficial in some areas and applying it across the board. I think it's good as an employee who spends as much time as I do on the road to cut costs where possible. I would want to hire someone like that. That's entirely different than accepting low end as a way to live life.

This lesson carries into so many other areas of my life as well... Sometimes I eat garbage food because it's cheaper than a healthy meal. Really what I'm doing every time I make the choice for the junk is telling myself I'm not worthy of the healthy choices. This is a great example, to sink in my point!

We could write "I am worthy" a zillion point five (5) times and it won't change anything until we are willing to truly look at our actions and what we are telling ourselves through them. In manifesting, actions are so much more powerful than written &/or spoken words. So, me being more aware of my actions, will give me that hunch into what I'm manifesting much quicker than anything I write or talk about.

In saying all of this, I'm so grateful for being crabby in Vegas last week, because it showed me how to grow into living the life of my highest visions. It showed me how my soul envisions my life. Thank you!!

Lessons Learned in Life: Health choice

Today I learned that fear is a natural part of certain times in my life. The larger lesson is that this fear can defeat me, or I can use the strength gained from feeling the fear to motivate me into action. The choice is entirely mine...

I've been having this issue going on for a month or so where no matter how much water I drink it doesn't fulfill my constant thirst. It seems like it started during my trip to Vegas. Although I didn't realize it at the time, I was buying four bottles of water each night because of how thirsty I felt all night. I just put it off to the dry climate. Now two weeks later, and back in Michigan, it hasn't changed, devouring as much water as my stomach will hold and still feeling thirsty. Up to six trips to the bathroom every night has me sleep deprived and unfocused. On top of this, I've lost almost (20) pounds in one and a half months.

Everything everyone tells me has the word diabetes tied to it... This word is what brought up the fear in me. Knowing that ignoring it builds the fear stronger, I allowed myself to feel the fear and ask, "How do you what this to go, Joe?"

In the past, something like this would leave me depressed and defeated. Even before I saw a doctor and found out what the problem was.

Tonight, I realized this situation has given me the opportunity to practice owning my Creatorship and I have to admit that I'm a little excited to apply my learnings into this situation. Now don't get me wrong, I do have an appointment with my doctor on Friday, because he will know how to explain the mechanics of my body, related to these symptoms better than I can understand on my own. Between this moment and then, I get to place my effort on knowing my health is perfect and that I can create a clean bill of health for myself, which I expect to confirm on Friday. I have something concrete to sink my teeth into, in proving to myself, my ability to determine the outcome of my life!

Actually, as I think more about this, regardless of the prognosis I receive from the doctor, all this is supposed to be in my path. I will find out why I brought this event into my life, what I'm supposed to learn from it and who I'm supposed to assist from this life lesson.

After the initial posting of this, I spoke to one of my two best male friends and he told me his nephew just had the same symptoms and it ended up being a bug...how cool is that? I come to a conclusion and instantly receive feedback supporting my choice... So Awesome!!

How awesome is this path?

Lessons Learned in Life: Gratitude

Today I learned more depth about gratitude. I've been talking for some time now about how grateful I am for my life. Gratitude for the people in my life. Even the people I used to look at through eyes of hatred, anger and disappointment. I'm grateful for the situations of my life. Even the situations I used to judge as bad or negative. Mainly because they have taught me my greatest lessons.

So, as I look at gratitude and how my life transformed, I remember a couple years ago I started to do a daily personal inventory every night and during this time of reflection, I would list out me gratitude's. Almost everyone has heard about a gratitude list, right? A list of things in our life we can pull up to help remind us of how good life is. It's important for me to have this list, although it's only part of the equation applied which lead to how I've come to find true happiness in my life.

The other portion of the work I did was to spend time reflecting on my day and being honest about how much time I spent during that day in my gratitude's versus how much time I spent trying to make something good, for instance, when I first started this process, I realized I would let my son spend hours watching television alone, while I sat on the phone trying to make a negative relationship positive. Now this is after spending a whole year and $15,000 fighting for 50% custody of his time.

Thank God I learned the benefits of self-honesty because without the capability of being honest with myself I would not of been able to realize I spent very little time living in my gratitude's and the time I did spent with them was spent trying my best to protect them, as my thinking back then was that can be taken from me. It stated out with an estimated 20% of my time living in my gratitude's versus 80% trying to produce gratitude in situations that did not hold any.

BUT IT WAS A STARTING POINT...

As things unfolded and circumstances unfolded, I would take a minute to ask myself "is this my gratitude or not." A simple yes or no answer. If it was something, I was grateful for, I kept going. If not, I would change what I was doing. It might not sound like much, but I can tell you my friend, it has pole vaulted me into a level of happiness I never knew existed. And it's self-feeding, because it grows my gratitude's when I focus on living in the areas that I'm already grateful for. At the same time, the things that happen that I'm not grateful for seem to vanish, which allows me more time for happiness!

 A real WIN/WIN we have here!!

Lessons Learned in Life: Release of Judgement

Today I learned how very grateful I am that, for whatever reason, I have this willingness to learn and to grow beyond my programming. This whole Creatorship is based on choice. I have choices every day, all day long. We all do. What follows pertains to the choices we are faced with about being a victim of life versus an amazing life being a constant blessing and lesson...

Granted, I am rounding the half century mark and it's taken this long for me to have the kahunas to even start to question the important questions about life, but frankly, I don't care. There is so much excitement in discovering the answers, the timing of it all isn't a factor. There is such an amazing thrill in realizing there really isn't judgment (good/bad, right/wrong, fair/unfair) and it's even more exciting to practice this principal in life and see the changes in outcomes first hand, that I've experienced.

Typically, I don't utilize this format to spew advice and I'm not intending to do so here either. What I would like to do is spell out a quick "what I do" just in case anyone wants to test it. And if you do, I'd love to hear back from you as to what results you receive! This one change has been pivotal in my awakening!

 At the on-start of a situation unfolding, ask yourself, "*If there is no right/wrong, no good/bad, no such thing as fair/unfair and life happens FOR me and not to me, why is this happening in my life?"*

 Sometimes it took a little bit of practice and persistence because the mind (ego) wants to keep fitting the situation into a judgement, which ultimately places us as a victim and that role immediately stops growth. I wrote a two-part post on forgiveness, where I hope I did a decent job explaining how the victim role cannot co-exist with 'Owning Our Creatorship.'

 Each time you become aware of a thought that has judgement, just keep bringing you're thinking back to 'LIFE HAPPENS FOR US, not to us, so why is this happening FOR ME.'

 It sometimes takes some time for the purpose of the event or situation to show up, but it always does. ALWAYS! What happens for me is the realizing of the purpose brings the exact insight I need to grow and move forward and for the awesomeness of life to open a little wider than it was prior.

And it has been this simple yet vital change that has been my gateway to a life of true happiness, true love, true spirituality... Truly OWNING MY CREATORSHIP!

I hope you try this exercise and I really hope to hear back from you. Whether it be your results, a sticking point that we can discuss or any other comments.

May you Own Your Creatorship!!

Lessons Learned in Life: Perception

Today I learned a lesson that although seemingly small, determines the outlook of my entire life!

Roughly three weeks ago I had a new kitchen floor installed. A floating linoleum floor. Love it! Looks like rectangular rough stone tile. Really dresses up the kitchen. For me personally, being able to afford installing a new kitchen floor represents another step in my manifesting abundance. Up until this point I would not have been able to do such a thing without letting other financial obligations go unpaid.

Ok, so today they are installing new carpet. Another exciting event, right?

Well guess what...

As I'm moving everything out of the front room in prep for the install, I dropped a large speaker on the kitchen floor and tore it. Right in a travel spot. When my floor guy arrived and inspected the tear, he told me he doesn't know how to repair it because it is floating. It sounds like the best he will be able to do is soften it, so it doesn't appear so clearly.

I'm sure you can imagine the initial upset in something like this happening. A bit of swearing, turns to anger which turns to taking it personal for making a mistake. Heck, I even apologized to my floor guy when he arrived...

Through this process which I am adding way too many words to explain (lol), come my lesson...

Once I took some time to have a coffee, stop kicking myself in the pants and calm my mind, I remembered a couple stories I've been given in the past that apply perfectly.

I remember a friend of mine shared these with me many years ago. When he told me these stories, I had no idea that 10-12 years later I would need this information as I do now.

The first story surrounds around a vacation he took to Hawaii. He was on the beach one evening watching the sunset. A littered cigarette butt discarded on the beach caught his attention. He described how pissed off he felt seeing that someone would garbage up the beach in that manner. That one piece of garbage was ruining his entire vacation...

Then it hit him....

He was letting this spec of imperfection ruin the most beautiful view he has ever experienced. He did end up getting to enjoy the sunset.

His second story was about a cracked tile in the foyer of his otherwise perfect condo. He purposely left the tile in the floor to remind him of life's imperfections. On his strong days he looked at the tile and saw its purpose. Other days he would look at the tile and want to replace it. On these days, he knew he had to practice acceptance of life being exactly as it's supposed to be.

Now I too have the gift of an imperfection that can remind me of how perfect life is, even with its imperfections. How awesome is that! In this moment I would still rather have the stories and the perfect floor, but I know that's not one of my choices...

My favorite prayer is the Serenity Prayer...

God, grant me the serenity to accept the things I cannot change,

Courage to change the things I can.

And the wisdom to know the difference...

Lessons Learned in Life: Trust

 T R U S T... Such a simple five letter word and at the same time has such a huge impact on every facet of our lives.

 Trust fits into everything we do as well as everything we choose not to do. It forms our beliefs, our ambition, our relationships, our career (or non-career), every nook and cranny of who we are. The other thing about trust is it seems like a tiny fracture to it can cause a lifetime of crippled ness.

 As part of my Owning Our Creatorship series, I believe distrust is the barrier that determines how far we advance with everything else. The more completely I allow myself to trust, the more my life is complete. It's a continuous, expanding circle, up to the point I choose distrust!

 So, knowing this, why would any of us choose dis-trust, one might ask (and I would thank the person for asking, because it leads to what follows...lol)? There are so many ways that distrust enters into us I could not possibly supply a full list. Heck, I wouldn't even expect I would know them all. What I have learned from my personal experiences is that regardless of the vehicle, it's how we process the event that makes all the difference.

There is the choice to be a victim vs. seeing how my choices called the event into fruition, ultimately leading to something I needed to learn in order to grow. Distrust can go all the way back to very early childhood, when a parent makes a promise and it's not kept, too much deeper things. I am not claiming to understand issues outside of my experience, only to relate how I've been able to reposition my view in order to remove my distrust and afford myself more happiness and contentment in my life, which ultimately affects everyone else in my life.

Another big one that I've personally dealt with is a habit related to expectations. This one has bitten me in the tail quite a bit. I have this character defect of placing my expectations of someone on them, instead of finding out through their actions who they really are. Then later down the line, when they are not meeting my expectations, I label it distrust.

Now, knowing all this and applying steps that help us to truly Own Our Creatorship are two completely different things. Both necessary, since without the knowing, there wouldn't be steps and without the steps, knowing would be fatal.

So, what I plan to do is...

First, be aware of the areas of my life I don't trust. Where it relates to people, ask myself if it is that person, or could it be me trying to plug my expectations into them. Actually, the same could be said for a majority of the other situations of my life as well.

Next would be to see if there is a rose in the area of distrust. What I mean by that is if there is a lesson, or valuable piece of information that I need to pick up on in order to grow. There usually is and finding the lesson helps so much to stop the continuous looping in relearning/re-experiencing.

Finally, the old saying "in order to trust, I have to be trustworthy" applies. It would be almost impossible to trust if I'm not living a trustworthy life.

I don't know if this will help clear up 100% of all trust issues, but I do know it helps me enormously in my life. Let me know if it helps you as well...

Lessons Learned in Life: Gratitude

(again :))

 Today I learned that gratitude is more a way of life, than anything else. Our gratitude grows to the extent that we allow it to.

 Looking back over my life, I've spent a lot of time wishing. Wishing my life were how I could envision it to be. Wishing I could obtain the level of success I felt I deserved. Wishing to be comfortable in my own skin. Wishing to have true friends and a loving relationship. Wishing I could earn more money than I spent. Nothing, absolutely nothing changed, no matter how much I tried to force aspects of my life to be different.

 Through a series of events, I was forced to stop wishing and start living. Instead of spending a majority of my day wishing and fantasizing, I had to start living moment to moment. It was either that or completely destroy myself. It got that bad.

 Little by little (and I mean that literally, a crumb at a time), I started to look at what was, rather than how I wanted everything to be. I started to notice more about who I was and who the people around me were. I started to recognize the fact that all my necessities were being met, regardless of my mindset at the time, telling me I would fail. Over the matter of seven years I grew to know myself very, very well. Life stopped being something to resent and became a blessing.

I woke up this morning and my first thought was that I've been the parent I've looked up to others for being through my sons' entire teenage life. I no longer have to wake up regretting my actions of yesterday. Life isn't something to be done through short cuts, scheming and scamming.

Today, I enjoy who I am and this allows me to enjoy others more. I don't have to resent, be jealous or envious of others. Because I've learned to be proud of who I am, I can be prouder of the people in my life that I love.

Today, I have the best job I've ever had. I'm not a big shot and don't have a fancy title, but I'm pretty successful at what I do and doing my job to the best of my ability adds to me gratitude. I have friends that I would drop everything for in a moment's notice and believe they would do the same for me.

Owning Our Creatorship means we can dislike a person's actions without throwing the person out of my life. We can enjoy the material things in my life, knowing we can be just as grateful about life without them. The owning comes in when life is lived for the experiences. Someone I really look up to says it best, whenever he says "life is about building memories."

 If anyone reads this and doesn't feel this awesome excitement about life, please reach out to me. If not me, please reach out to someone. LIFE IS NOT MEANT to be miserable. I would love nothing better than an opportunity to share what's been shared with me. I talk in terms of Owning Our Creatorship as my movement. But at the bottom of it all, it's the sharing with others that increases happiness and gratitude in our lives!!

Lessons Learned in Life... Blessed is a choice

Today I'm learning life is filled with blessings. They swarm us constantly, to the point of overwhelming gratitude. I'm learning how to allow them to penetrate my heart and soul.

It seems like all areas of my life are growing with blessings. Not just material things, but they are included as well. It's the daily feeling of not only truly knowing myself but enjoying my own company. It's traveling for business and being able to relax, all by myself. And at the same time feeling the depth of love in the relationships in my life. It's a feeling or knowing that everything is in perfect order.

What's amazing is that I'm able to feel like this way in one of the toughest emotional years I've had, with my Dad passing in January, recently finding out I have diabetes, and experiencing a close friend crashing due to addiction. Revisiting the perfect order thought, as much as I miss him, I know Dad is in a better place and his spirit lives amongst us. My diagnosis is helping me to finally learn and practice healthy eating. My friend is reaching out and allowing God to save their life.

All this hit me the other night, while talking to a friend on the phone. In sharing gratitude about life, he commented, "I can't wait until I hit that point, of having good things show up for me." This is exactly how I used to see things. I'll be happy when I get (fill in the blank) ...

My gratitude started back when I was paying out more money every month than I had coming in. I would have to utilize a credit card to grocery shop the weeks I had my son. I struggled to find $20 for work money week after week. I was paying child support, spousal support, health insurance and major Visa debt because a judge told me I would. My support team would not let me file bankruptcy because they said I had to experience trusting God to help me fulfill my obligations. I was not in a relationship, or in unhealthy relationships. It was while living like this that I was taught to be grateful. To feel the blessings God was bestowing upon me. To trust that if I could relinquish even a splinter of my fear, my faith would grow by forests.

Several years later... I was able to purchase my dream bike last week. A 2014 Harley Davidson Street Glide Special. Absolutely Awesome!! At the same time, the bike in itself isn't the gift. It's the experiences or memories that really have me excited. The ride to Ohio & New York with a friend in June. The experience of jumping on it this summer and riding to whatever campground I end up at. My 3,500-mile ride from Arizona back to MI in the fall.

And most of all, it's in knowing that if the bike went away, if the job changes or whatever may happen in 'life to come' I will have all my needs met, well beyond what I can imagine. We all do. All we have to do is to choose to shift our focus. Find one thing to consider a blessing and then another and pretty soon they will start to pop up automatically... I dare you to try it!

Lessons Learned in Life: People Pleasing and the way out!

 Although it's been a while since I last posted, the lessons just keep on a coming'...

 Just recently, another layer of the onion that is me has been peeling. It came about from the role of people pleasing. This has been something I've struggled with even before I knew the words or their meaning. I spend a large portion of my life doing things for others or helping others, not because of a choice towards charity, but because I felt like I had to do so.

 As I grew older and started to realize the depth of lack of fulfilment my life had become (and many payments to counsellors), I started to see how much of my life I gave away in order to feel accepted by someone. One of the best lessons I received in understanding this happened a little over a year ago...

 I was seeing a counselor, ultimately in the attempt to make a negative relationship good. It failed, as it should have, but I kept going individually to see this counselor and gained more in that few months than I had all the other counselors I've seen combined. Anyways, back to the story...

As I sat in her office one afternoon, she complimented me on my watch. I thanked her, but she went on for another minute or so about how nice it was. She asked me to hand it to her. Without thinking, I unbuckled the clasp and handed it to her. She laughed. I looked confused.

She explained to me that the watch symbolized my life and she symbolized the kind of women I attract into my life. They ask for areas of my life and I immediately hand it over to them. I've lived my life in this manner enough to cripple my understanding to differentiate between what is healthy vs unhealthy for ME.

This event lit a bulb within me. Anytime I saw Amy after that, she would somehow through the conversation ask for my watch, wallet or something and I would say no. Initially, realizing the game I was abrupt in my response (which was growth for me, making the switch from being suicidal to homicidal) and eventually being able to say no in as kind a manner as possible.

Just having this understanding has helped me immensely to recognize within myself when I'm playing a role to please someone else and when

I'm living healthy. I can offer to help and feel good about it. I never knew that aspect of helping someone else existed.

Another benefit, or gift of all this is that it seems the more I practice healthy "Yes's & No's" the fewer people are popping up in my life who need the kind of person who people pleases. My healthy relationships are growing and the unhealthy ones and getting right sized (as they say in the business world)!

All I have to do is decide if I'm willing to give my watch away :)

As I write this, I'm realizing how much I miss spending this time opening my heart to share! I hope someone gets something out of this writing and if God willing, shares back!

Lessons Learned in Life: Dealing with Resentments

 I feel compelled to start by thanking everyone for their comments to my last writing. Funny, I started all this hoping to touch others and it took me taking a break in writing/sharing to understand the impact all this is having, as well as an added appreciation of the comments I've received from day one. Warms my heart!! Today's lesson surrounds around my connection to God. I have relearned that I cannot have a secure, intimate, close relationship with God at the same time I'm choosing to let anger, resentment and/or fear rule my emotions.

 Another area the choice to feed judgment and negativity effects is my ability to look at my life with clear vision. I practice taking a daily inventory of my life, to do my best to keep my side of the street clean and make restitution where necessary. Believe me, I fall short of being perfect on this, every single day, day after day. But in making the effort, I know so much more about myself and am constantly learning more. I've had this ongoing situation where I'm choosing to pick up stress, anger and resentments. Not intentional mind you. It's been developing over the past couple weeks and although not exploding, has a pretty good boil to it. During this time, I'm noticing a feeling of disconnect with God and my daily inventories seem more blaming and quietly attacking than a good view of my life and my part.

This past weekend I decided I didn't want to go through this upcoming week feeling stressed out and angry. Even though I made the decision, those feelings stayed with me through the weekend and into Monday. I worked and the feelings were there. I went to the gym and they tagged along. After the gym I jumped in the shower (with the anger & resentment) before I headed out again.

As I was toweling off, I had this feeling to sit for a few minutes. The feeling actually carried a ten-minute period with it. I did. I sat in a chair in my bedroom. As I sat there, clarity came over me. I started to recognize the flowers in the backyard. Then I noticed the way the tress is starting to blossom. I even noticed the anger, fear and resentments being minimized. The more I let this feeling control my actions and thinking the more of my blessings came to mind. The highest thought I had was God speaking to me. Not an audible voice, but a feeling. You know the one, it comes from deep in the chest and instantly overrides all thoughts. It said, "Everything, absolutely everything in life is going to be perfect. Just believe that."

Now mind you, I didn't ask for this. I wasn't praying like mad for God to step in and fix something. As I stated, I was angry, pissed off and growing rapidly in resentments.

As I became more aware of my surroundings, I felt love more than any other feeling. Not suddenly, but in a smoothing kind of way, I could look back at over the past couple weeks and realize I have a lot going on. My son is graduating high school and moving in a couple months. I'm hosting his graduation party. I am about to put my house up for sale. My plans for my next step in life are not clearly showing themselves yet. On top of all this, I have been in the process of evaluating a long-term relationship to determine its healthiness for all parties.

With all this whirling around at the same time, how could I possibly expect to have the ability (of my own accord) to take an accurate inventory? And If I'm unable to inventory myself, how can I keep a close connection to a life-giving source?? It's impossible. Ultimately, what I was doing was spending a majority of my work day stressed to the point that I haven't been as active as I should be. I've been choosing fear in place of action towards the graduation party. I've been trying to stuff fear, instead of admitting it and letting it go. I've been acting somewhat honest, where people's futures are being based on my words. The final word I have to say about all this is Thank God that seeking for me doesn't mean I go out and find. Seeking, to me, means I become open to… Open to receiving. Open to allowing. Open to paying attention to those little inner whispers that carry a direction and open to following that direction.

Lessons Learned in Life: Character

Actually, my lesson started a few days ago while re-reading a book I've read several times, cover to cover. You know, that book that you use as your life's reference manual? It could be the Bible for some, the actual book title isn't important.

The initial writing of this blog started on May 21st. This whole subject of character building has been a constant unfolding up to this publishing. I'm finding this to be probably the most complex subject of study I've come across. It touches every aspect of my life. Internally it is directly linked to my self-esteem. I'm realizing that my character, or lack of, parallels throughout all my relationships.

As I was reading, I came across an area that spoke about character building. It stated that although most of us talk about wanting to build character, when it comes between building true character or comfort, the majority chooses comfort. That got me thinking about my own life.

More specifically about what areas of my life am I settling for comfort because I'm either afraid to choose the path of building character, or it's easier to be comfortable. So far, I'm realizing fear are more times than not, my reason for choosing the comfort although I am clearly being shown the times when it's just been easier to choose comfort over the work of building character.

Typically, when I fear an outcome I would not enjoy, it's easier to pacify the situation by going along with, or not standing my ground as to what I know, need or believe.

I find I'm asking myself questions such as, "Where am I choosing to be 'almost' completely honest?" This has been a more prominent theme throughout my adult life than I want to admit. Instead of being completely honest in situations, I leave out a portion of truth to allow me wiggle room later on. I've sold myself on the reason for this dishonesty is to help the other person in some way, or not to come across as hurtful or a hundred other good lines of BS, but the full truth honesty seems to always come down to selfishness of some type on my part.

Another huge lesson I've learned that really helps guide me is that true character doesn't limit what I say. The desire to build character helps immensely in how I say things, but I haven't found any subjects to be taboo.

I expect there to be more coming on this subject!

Lessons Learned in Life: Ask & It Shall Be Given

Well hello All! I've so much missed this part of my life!

Ok, so here is am. I now live in an apartment in Iowa, 474 miles away from my previous home in Michigan. I'm settling into a new place, new job and what should be new discoveries all around me.

It seems like it's all happened in the blink of an eye...

In all the shuffle of my son graduating and relocating to Arizona, his graduation party, me accepting a new position, finding a place to live, listing and selling my home, finding a home, packing, moving and unpacking, all in a matter to two months it's no wonder that my mind (and body) have been moving at a pace that feels quicker than the speed of light!

So, as I'm reaching the tail end of completing this portion of my life puzzle, moving forward from things that I've tried my heart to, I've been feeling lost. I have been doing what I do best with it all, spitting it out to anyone that will listen. This seems to bring some immediate relief, but nothing that lasts for much longer than the hiccups...

I've continued my soul journey to the best of my ability. Working via satellite with my great teacher on a regular basis. I've checked out local churches searching for substance, definition, clarity... Something!

Sunday while breathing and working with my breath worker, she asked me such a simple question... She asked, "Have you asked your spirit (God) why you are here, in this place right now?" I blew over it quickly, to get to the real issue of her helping me to figure out the answers to my questions. Later that evening, while scanning the TV, I came across Joyce Myers, and she was saying how before we bring our issues to other people, we ought to bring them to God first. Coincidence? I think not.

So, in going to bed I said as simply as possible, "*God, in seeing the unfolding of the reasons from all the travels you've led me through so far in my life, I know you have me here for a reason. Please reveal your love and your direction for my life. Please open my spirit to see the purpose.*" It hit me hard and I started to cry from the overwhelming ness of it.

 That question has opened my soul to hope, to the belief that even though it doesn't yet make sense to me, it will...

 So, for the past two months, I've been traveling around feeling empty, drained, sad, lonely & alone. Today I go to work and have a meeting with a guy and the conversation leads to God.
Imagine that, a fellow co-worker that I'm able to discuss our faith together. Not only that, he told me about a person starting a church with a unique way to open the door to God. So, wouldn't you know it, I'm out and about tonight, minding my own business and BAM... I happen to run into the gentleman who started the church.

 Overall, I don't know if the plan is I to assist him, but I do know that my heart is completely open to following my soul's path. I know that by asking my soul, my God my questions, it not only brings me more satisfying answers, but it frees me from me!

Lessons Learned in Life: Love without conditions (part I)

Today I am learning about love without conditions... A tough lesson for me as it is so wide-spread into all facets of life.

It seems the more I study the meaning of unconditional love, the less likely it is that I can ever experience it in its totality, while I live here on earth. In expecting unconditional love as the goal, similar to being Jesus-like, what I can manifest and bring into my life is to help others to raise their awareness of self-love, and allow others to assist me in raising my level of completeness and self-love. But I must be open to the message, which is to say that I must have self-forgiveness and ultimately realize that I never was wrong, bad, and incomplete in any way shape or form.

Any feelings of being incomplete, unlovable, less than, are all facades I create out of fear. Fear is the top-level emotion that opposes love. Love will always have the absence of fear and fear will always carry the absence of love. My lesson is in learning how I can purposely choose how I view myself and ultimately where my fears are. I've been taught this is a big part of self-realization. I am learning that I must take responsibility for healing my own wounds in order to get out of my vicious cycle of guilt and shame. I further understand teachers will continue to show up in my life to assist me in my journey to Own My Creatorship (I've missed that term!!). This world isn't meant to be walked alone.

 So, at this point in my lesson, I am working on the self-realization portion. I expect as my lesson unfolds it will carry me into the avenues where the healing takes place, which I can't wait to share. But for now, I feel hopeful that by focusing on knowing I have the responsibility to heal my wounds and understanding it starts with being honest with my man in the mirror, without judgement, that everything will unfold exactly as it's supposed to!

Lessons learned in life: Anger & Resentment

 Today I was brought the lesson of dealing with anger... Similar to cancer, it causes the most harm to the carrier...

 I grew up believing men were supposed to be tough. They fight, protect and from what I saw anger created fear in others and the guys who created the most fear were the most respected. This was based on a 10 years old child's view of the world. It was neat in my teen years but I realize now that I carried it much further into my adult life than I even recognized. This thinking got me beat up. A LOT! Sometimes by the same person multiple times.

 For a long time, anger became a way of life for me. The deeper I went into allowing anger to run my life, the darker my world became. Ultimately, the more of a victim I saw myself as, the less my life became mine. It was owned guided and directed through anger & resentment.

 As my enlightenment began 15 years or so ago, my beliefs about fear driven respect began to be overtaken by a respect for people I met that could be stern but kind. People that would stand

Up against something without crushing, yelling or criticizing. As this realization unfolded, which for me was a true spiritual awakening, I started to practice not being angry. This acting as if led to me almost exploding over simple things on numerous occasions. I could for a short period of time brush off the anger, act as if I didn't feel resentful, but what I didn't realize until after exhaustive measures on my part was that it's impossible to act as if I'm not angry. Literally impossible.

Through my trial period of controlling my anger I experienced migraine headaches, chest pain, extra weight and sugar issues from overeating. All in my best efforts to utilize self-control to not feel angry or resentful towards someone or something. My best efforts would have killed me if my thresh hold for pain were any greater! Thank God I'm not as strong as I want to be or thought I was!

Through growth, eventually I gained enough self-esteem to ask these people that I began to respect for their abilities to deal with situations without using anger as their opening statement, how they were able to achieve such a miraculous feat? They gave me the precious gift of the following four steps.

1- At the on-sight of any situation that had the potential of igniting anger, take a deep breath and exhale. A simple deep breath. Later I realized taking that deep breath put me in control of my thoughts, instead any programmed responses. The choice to take that breath gave me just that... A CHOICE!

2- Take a second breath and ask myself what it is about the situation that is touching on this part of myself. Might sound silly, but I almost guarantee it that fear of some sort will be behind it. The other culprit will be ego (which in itself is fear, so the guarantee stands :)) So I place my efforts on determining the fear within me that is touched on by whatever the situation I'm in at the moment.

3- Now that I am owning my thoughts and controlling my actions (instead of that instant reaction within me) I am better able to make the final determination on how I decide I want to respond to the situation.

There are times for me when I decide to act in an angry manner. Maybe that choice is because I'm not a saint, or maybe it's because, like Jesus Christ turning tables over in His Father's house, the situation calls for such action. What I do know is the number of times I have to review my actions to determine if I'm being the man, I want to be are fewer than I ever remember. I haven't experienced a migraine in quite some time now and my sugar and eating are healthier than they been for 20 years. I haven't been beat up in a long, long time.

The other benefit I'll leave you with is that I have found that no matter what is going on around me, using these steps allows me to be in control of myself. Someone can be whirling out of control and it doesn't knock me off balance.

Lessons Learned in Life: Change without Battling

Today I was confronted with my fighting my life.

It was brought to my attention this evening how much I am fighting life. I thought I was done with this, but I'm not. It goes all the way back to 12 years old, when I misunderstood what he meant when my dad told me I needed to toughen up. He was trying to address me being over sensitive. I heard that I needed to fight more and fight better.

This fighting carried into so many areas of my life. I realize that I continue to fight as part of receiving healing or growth. As part of accepting change. My whole life, there always had to be a physical enemy in order for me to let out my fear or the demons within me.

Looking right now, I've continually appointed someone who is doing me wrong, in order to make changes in my life. Rarely have I instituted a change in my life for ME. It's usually been against someone.

I haven't been aware of this role playing or even the need for change to include a battle.

Appointing the position of attacker has put the whole process into a position I've been able to comprehend so that I can go do my part for the change to infiltrate my life. Actually, the whole process has been based on an untruth that change requires a battle.

SO HERES THE QUESTION...

What if I didn't need the attacker or the enemy?

Or better yet, what if I have been my persecutor all along? Which is really the case for any of us in this type of situation, isn't it?

What if I were to allow or accept change in my life just for the sake of bringing more happiness and love for myself as well as those around me?

What if??

Lessons Learned in Life: Love

In my search for fulfilling my mantra, "I am the man I want me to be" I have touched on an area I have not experienced thus far in my travels...

This whole battle lesson is bringing more light into the idea of change coming about through peaceful means, something completely new to me. All based on a simple question, "What if there didn't have to be an enemy?"

What if I came all the freaking way to Iowa, to be told by a group of guys that don't even really know me, that they love me? And what if the lesson in hearing this would be to challenge my incorrect beliefs about love? To dig down to the minuscule fibers of the root of my untruth.

The untruth that love has to be built over time. That love is something only shared through deep relationships. What if maybe, love really is abundant and free for each of us, to give in unlimited supply to each other, regardless if we think and act alike.

Further, what if love is an instant decision where we can choose to give and receive at any moment, under any circumstances and are only limited by the amount of our choice? What if love isn't supposed to be saved for only certain people our paths cross?

To witness love from someone willing to take the time to spend talking to me about all this and being willing to speak up with words that were obviously spiritual intervention seems to be evidence of this possibility. Along with the uncountable number of people that have been showing me the same example through my entire life. Even before I realized they were doing so!

This brings me to an affirming prayer... God, I want change and it's possible without having to feel the victim or without a battle, please show me! Please help me to know love as you intend it to be and please help me to see your loving will for me!!

What if...
Love is free & unlimited
Love is strangers as well as the most intimate relationships
Love is peace and calmness
Love is the absence of fear & lack
AND MY GOD SAYS "IT IS ALWAYS!"

What if...
We don't have to fight for love
We don't have to battle to find or give love
We don't have to earn love
We don't have to struggle
AND MY GOD SAYS, "WE DON'T EVER AGAIN!!"

Lessons Learned in Life: Thrive in my "singleness"

My untruth has always been 'that a single person is a lonely person'. So, it would make sense that finding myself single would bring about feelings of loneliness.

I have made the bold decision that I AM NOT GOING TO LIVE IN THIS UNTRUTH!

I feel like I'm supposed to break this writing down into sections... Let's see how it works out...lol

Untruth-
That I'm alone & have no one to love me.
That I'm either too heavy, don't dress "right" have a flawed personality, joke around too much.
That I'm less than or not worthy (both from birth & based on some wrong I've committed).

These are the thoughts that want to take control of my thinking... But SCREW THAT!

The real truth-

If I really look at my life in this moment, I'm enjoying a Dunkin Donuts coffee (the best coffee EVER), sitting on a balcony in the morning sunshine in Gilbert Arizona, visiting my Mom.

I spend at least a couple nights a week with friends I have made in Iowa.

Relationships with like-minded people are showing up constantly in my life.

I have vacationed in Alaska with my favorite person in the world. My son!

I have been able to located & visit my favorite place in the world (thus far) ... UTAH!

I am currently fulfilling a lifelong goal of learning to play the guitar.

I get massages on a bi-weekly basis, regularly work with my breath master, and recently have committed to working with a coach that is further assisting me in stepping into my dream life. We met during my visit to Utah, which would not have happened if my life situation were not as it is.

Oh, and I'm taking voice lessons. I will kick ass mimicking Aerosmith at some point on the old' karaoke machine! lol

And that's really the bottom line... My life could not unfold as it is or as it needs to if my situation were any different than it is in this moment!

As I review the lists above, I have to smile at how weak the untruths really are in comparison to all the blessings I get to choose. I also feel a sense of gratitude that the blessings unfold, even when my thinking is stuck in lack or untruths.

It would be so AWESOME to build a singles network. Not for the typical purpose of finding another single to unite, but to support each other in our singleness.

Whether you're in the untruths and need support, or on top of the world with thriving being single, please leave a comment and let's see if we can't pull this together and expand love, support & kindness to a healthy single soul.

Lessons Learned in Life: CONCLUSION

 With regards to my mission for Life's-Lessons, what a great word, Conclusion... The end of suffering.

 Actually, looking at the word through my spiritual studies, the word conclusion is the same as "rebirth" in that at the end of the conclusion state is always a new beginning.

 Before we dive into this one, I wanted to discuss 'untruths'. For me, an untruth is a thought or belief that I utilize to define an area of life that does not serve me in regards to unconditional love, spiritual growth or any other area of my life where I feel I keep running into a wall. If you're like me, you have spent some amount of your life living in untruths based on how you interpreted events from childhood. Right? For myself, trust was something I didn't learn very well growing up, so I've spent time in my adult life confused &

judging people through the vision of that child I was and my perceived outcome of the events I experienced, versus trusting my instincts.

Events happened and we didn't know to ask for clarification. On top of that, whatever or whoever delivered the event didn't know to clarify or protect us from accepting the message in a manner that was harmful to our self-esteem, vision of ourselves, or trusting in unconditional love. Heck, even "Who God is" was given to us.

All this was done in either our best interest or as a result of someone else's internal battle. Whatever the reason, the item I want to focus on here is that none of these influences have to matter.

WE HAVE A CHOICE!!

As an example of applying conclusion to something recently, the last posting was about singleness. I attempted to express about the frustration with the inner battles over being enough without being in a relationship.

Because of my beliefs that single people are lonely, not lovable, broken and all the rest of the crap, I had to be all those things. It only makes sense that if I'm single I am what I believe that state of being to be.

Then comes the conclusion... The new beginning...

The long list of things I GET TO enjoy being single that I would not, in the same way, if I were in a relationship. (If you haven't read it, I hope that you do so...) My conclusion is that it's an opportunity to discover who God is and who you are on a very individual basis.

Ok, enough about singleness...

My point in this article is that with every conclusion, there is a new beginning. Every untruth you are willing to look at, from where it developed to how it's holding you back today, holds a new, more exciting start in its hands.

Our willingness to grow is all that is to unclench the fingers for the hand of a new beginning to open wide. Whether you have experienced the conclusion/rebirth state in your life or are struggling with those inner battles, we are all in this together :)

Lessons Learned in Life: Self Will

 A few weeks I had the incredible privilege of riding my Harley Davidson Street glide Special across country! One of my bucket list items coming to fruition! Me & a good friend of mine left the Quad Cities on Friday, July 17th, not to be seen again around home until Saturday, July 25th... so I thought!!

 In order to avoid going through a moment by moment account of the trip (although for anyone who enjoys the freedom of living a week in the mountains with nothing more than a motorcycle, travel bag strapped to the back a few hundred in cash and 3 visa cards (to ensure funds did not become an issue), I am more than willing to elaborate in as much detail as one could stand... lol

 So, getting to the lesson. I have dedicated the past several years to understanding, developing growing and sharing about my God Within. Christians refer to it as the Holy Spirit, which I believe it to be. Buddhism refers to it as "The God Within" which to me is the same. Regardless of what religion defines that inner connection, all the areas I've studied all break it down to that inner connection to something greater than self.

Intuition is another common word I've heard & utilized to describe the God within me, or my soul.

Getting back to the story, the overall trail was through Iowa & Nebraska, into Colorado (Estes Park down to Buena Vista, up to Aspen, then south to Poncho Springs, south west through Durango and million-dollar highway of 550 and into Utah for the second half the trip). Like last year's trip, we end up adding more and more as we traveled. Packing too much in is so easy to do when up against a timeframe.

Now, I've spent a lot of time sharing about the incredible spiritual lessons I've been learning over the past couple years. Things like how I've felt that inner spirit leading me and all the awesome things that have come about based on shutting my mind of and being, versus doing life. I believe that I have been what I might call a bit too confident in my abilities to set down self-will and follow the direction from that inner quite voice. This came in a very clear message on July 21st, 8:00 pm mountain time. A lesson that I pray lives with me the rest of my life...

We left Poncho Springs, CO around 8:30 am to head to Moab, Utah (where we planned the remainder of our trip before heading back to Iowa on Friday).

 This was about a 300-mile trip, expected to last around 5-7 hours with stops. When we left the hotel, I did my normal praying, asking God "to please keep us safe through the day's journey." Once we arrived in Durango, we stopped in at a local Harley dealership, bought the normal shirt souvenirs and I was talking to a guy working there who told me about the million-dollar highway. I instantly added this to our agenda for the day. (He did say that people come from all over the world to ride that trek.) Quick calculation showed we would still be in Utah by 8:30 pm, more than enough time to avoid night riding and possible deer encounters.

 Now remember, I'm still very confident that my inner spirit is leading me, even though I felt that slight hesitation (WARNING 1) about adding the extra miles to the daily ride. So off we went...

 At one of our photo shoots stops we met a brother biker who rode up from Louisiana, was on a three-week trip to end in Sturgis for the annual biker convention. During our conversation, about comparing travels, he was surprised we were planning on traveling all the way to Moab that day. (WARNING 2), I immediately dismissed what he said, thinking "If I had the time available that you do, of course I would go at a slower pace." We ended up seeing him two other spots along the day. Once on top of a mountain where we stopped to have lunch, overlooking the most picturesque view of mountains, roads & rivers all co existing I have ever had the privilege of seeing. This fellow biker asked again if we altered our plans (WARNING 3), this one had me thinking.

Looking back, that inner voice spoke at a louder volume than I can remember feeling/hearing before. As self-will gets stronger and more stubborn, the easier it is to ignore the inner spirit. And my mind can be so convincing, as at that time I felt like My decision to go forward was still being led by my God!! The final time we saw this gentleman, he was parked outside a hotel, unloading his gear from his bike for the night.
That was around 5:30 or 6:00 in Silverton, CO (175 miles, 3 hours away from Moab). (WARNING 4).

There were at least two other things that happened that were telling me to stop and get back on God's time, instead of mine. But I just knew we needed to get to Moab! And we needed to do so before dark, so we didn't have to worry about some unlikely encounter with deer, or worse, Elk!!

While speeding along at the posted speed of 55 miles per hour on Highway 90, at approximately 8:00 (40 minutes outside Moab), a deer jumped out on the road about even with my front tire, stopped for a fraction of a moment and lunged right into the side of me! I'm not sure if his impact broke my leg or if it was the steel bar in the ground holding a reflector that one of the two of us hit hard enough to bend to the ground. My bike was forced off the road and into the shallow ditch where it went down, slid out of the ditch across a gravel road and into the ditch on the other side. I stopped less than two feet shy of a wooden fence post and barb wire. My bike was mangled and pieces of it scattered all around the area from the point of contact with the deer to its landing point, 50-70 feet away.

I never lost consciousness, which I can tell ya, is pretty weird to see a live deer, gravel and weeds travel so quickly before my eyes. Other than a broken leg, I have a shoulder that will require reattachment of the bicep, reattachment of the rotator cuff to the shoulder and a level 3 tear repair of the rotator cuff. Also, I now have a new level of appreciation for anyone who experiences a gravel scrub bath!!

Even through this self will run riot, I was blessed beyond belief... for instance, if the whole event happened 100 yards either direction, instead of a shallow ditch and gravel, I would have been sent down a deep ditch with scattered boulders... The only house around was across the street from the accident and housed the town's EMT... It could have been a larger deer or Elk... I could have experienced life altering head injuries due to not wearing a helmet.

As I tried my best to lay around the hotel on Wednesday, so I could be driven to Salt Lake City, Thursday for a flight back to Iowa, I kept thinking about all the little signs I avoided, at which point I could clearly see how I had tricked myself into following my plan instead of following that inner spirit. I carry a lot of gratitude for how strong that intuition has grown to be and a new appreciation for strength my own will can have in my choices. It reminds me to slow down, spend more time in being and to count my blessings more often than I have been!!

Lessons Learned in Life... Purpose

 Today I learned that uncertainty is a part of normal life. Here I sit at 6:00 on a Sunday evening. The first time I've been able to drive onto my two acres of wooded property in Iowa. I'm sitting here in a campfire chair, overlooking the valley, hoping to get a glimpse of wildlife. As I allow myself to absorb the quiet tranquility feeling that all familiar shift from thinking to feeling, I hold the last remanences of a question that has been visiting my mind more and more often...

 What is my life for, it's purpose? If God saved me from dying in that motorcycle accident because he has work for me, what *is* the work??

 I am going to try an experiment here... I am going to allow myself some time sitting here to transform from thinking to feeling. The following words will come from that part of my being, unedited. I am going into this with the questions above, seeking direction. Let's see what happens.

 My life is not a task list to be accomplished. I am not here for a single purpose; I am here for all things. I am no more a teacher than I am a student. I am a prophet as much as a pauper. My life's purpose is to live life. To learn how to fully live and to share that with others. My fortune to amass is in the leaves that quietly sway with the wind before me. My treasure is in being part of this moment. I somehow feel this connection to the trees around me. These are the things that bring calmness to my heart and excitement my soul.

Similar to the many accomplishments I place so much importance in, I could walk down further into the woods, but I don't need to. I am perfectly placed exactly where I am in this moment. God will guide me. He will guide my direction and my life. Similar to the driveway from the road to the pad on this property, it will have its shares of hills. It will bend right to left and back again. It will have bumps, along with smooth spots. But I can be rest assured that it will bring an awesomeness that I could not have imagined. This I already know. I have tasted the fruit of following His will.

As the woods begin to darken, there is one small tree, surrounded by a thick forest of larger trees, towering way above it. This tiny sapling is reflecting enough sunlight to light up the area around it. Of the entire area, it is the only one lit up by the sun. A thought, "Maybe I'm that tree. Maybe each of us is that tree." Within moments the light of that tree is gone. Could it be that it was intentionally held by the light for that brief length of time for me to understand my own human significance? Overwhelming thought, but believable!

All around me is life. All around me is death. Neither is more of less beautiful than the other. My eyes view green and yellow and white. I see strong tall healthy trees as well as young. I also see a beautiful tall tree, stripped of its leaves, its bark falling from it. Its branches look so brittle. Yet it stands tall in its death. Somehow it seems proud. Proud of its contribution to life, or proud for the life it led. Even after its death, it draws respect and gratitude.

As I conclude this writing so that I can spend time strictly absorbing, I am not sure if I will build a house on this property or if it's something, I will hold onto just to protect my availability of being here. What I do know is that this ground is spiritual. How often does a guy get to enjoy a two-acre, wooded church surrounded by valley? :)

Lessons Learned in Life: Overthinking

S T O P!

Itis really that easy. It does not seem like it, but we have control over our thinking. It might not seem like it, but we have a choice each and every moment on what we think about.

How awesome is it that we get to determine which thoughts we allow and which we do not? Something completely different from emotions, even though it doesn't always seem like it.

WE GET TO CHOOSE!

I believe this is the start of something huge!

Lessons Learned in Life: My 30-Day Reprieve

 For whomever may come across this article, I am trying something a bit different...

 Over the past few weeks I have been feeling like I am being called to put my practices into play in my life. With the recent passing of my friend and mother, life seems different, as I would assume it would for everyone else who has lost their second parent. I am realizing life is different. I am different. I cannot yet describe exactly how, but there is this sense of who I am as an individual is restructured or altered.

 Anyway, this calling comes from within my chest a that I have mentioned in other writings. It is leading me to detach. Not in an unhealthy way. Quite the opposite actually. I have decided as of midnight tonight, which will be November 1st, I am withdrawing from television, radio, reading and instead am going to spend my time being active and purposeful in my life. I am going to shop and cook my food, in place of all the eating in restaurants all the time.

 I will be updating through posts on a regular

basis throughout November, but I am not planning on sending an email update for each posting, except when a life lesson comes into play.

I am, excited and for whatever reason a bit nervous about taking this on, but let us see why I am drawn to this and its purpose.

Lessons Learned in Life: Day One of 30 Day Reprieve

Getting ready for bed after Day 1! Today was different from my previous Sundays.

For one, I had to remind myself countless times today that I already have everything I need within me to thrive through this process. I had to remind myself of this when a Sunday program I typically watch came on TV. I again had to remind myself of this when I sat idle too long and wanted to grab hold of my go-to book that I continually refer to as a spiritual lift or reminder. I just kept telling myself that I have everything I need without going outside myself to live a happy healthy life today.

Today I started in meditation and prayer, following by stretching and about a two (2) mile walk/jog. I admit much more walking than jogging. Now that I have the green light on moving my arm, after having my bicep and rotator cuff reattached to my shoulder; it is rehab time. Not my favorite activity, but the stretching is gaining me mobility.

For whatever reason, I am now taking up sketching. Not sure of the reason for it, but I am following the guide within and that seems to be where it is leading me. I have finished my very first sketched mountain scene today. I utilized multiple shades of lead and even charcoal, not that I can tell the difference. I do have a new respect for people who are skilled at shading! My mountains look like Halloween scare fest when I finally decided to pull the pencil off the paper. But in this, I found a couple hours of peace and solitude.

I cooked all my meals today and talked on the phone more than usual, which is typically a lot already. I did decide to alter my path by allowing "non-teaching" reading. Reading for entertainment. *A Walk in The Woods*, by Bill Bryson. I am four (4) chapters in and enjoying the heck out of it!

My spiritual message today was gifted to me today while breathing with my spiritual teacher and soul sister Paula Rowe of Soulawakeningproject.com... "Masters do not teach. They raise the vibrational frequency of life consciousness."

Lessons Learned in Life... Day Five of 30 Day Reprieve

Seems as though I experienced some technical difficulties... Thanks to the efforts of Derek Sands of Botec Design (www.Botecdesign.com) I'm up and running again!!

Today is day 5! Seeming a bit more challenging than I suspected. In regards to the distractions from outside influence, such as the television, radio and reading are things I feel like I'm missing more than I expected. But they are far from being most of my struggle.

Surprisingly to me, the thing I'm struggling with most is living in my head. Thoughts. Thoughts about everything are constantly consuming my time. I noticed last night an hour and a half flew by with me sitting in my chair and thinking. Thinking about living arrangements, work, life, money, family, toys, should I buy, should I sell, should I buy to sell... Endless thoughts about things I cannot do anything about or that don't matter.

I am sharing this because I'm a real person, trying to live up to a challenge I've put before myself. I read a lot from the people I consider my spiritual mentors and its pissing me off that I've never read anything about them struggling like I am with this. The honest people in my life that have gone this path are sharing with me everyone taking on this type of thing run up against this. I want anyone else who may try something of this nature to know that when they run into this, it's normal. Just keep pushing forward... Remember how many times Jesus was tempted and just keep going.

Lessons Learned in Life: Day Eight of 30 Day Reprieve

 On day eight (8) I'm working to bring meditative thoughts into as much of my daily activities as possible...

 Although I was not able to spend as much time in a meditative state as my mind thinks I should, there were not any situations I found myself in that I wasn't able to handle with a serene state. So, from that regard, I'm going to call it a successful day.

 I lived where my hands were...

Lessons Learned in Life: Day 10 of 30-Day Reprieve

 Today marks 1/3rd of the way to the thirty (30) day mark!

  I am still struggling with feeling like I'm not doing this the right way or covering enough ground, but I am starting to see that as my expectations working against me. The insights are starting to show up in spite of my thoughts.

 I wrote this earlier without thought and wanted to capture it...

 This month is where I will find the strength to build on being the Man I was, into the Man I am. For me to step out and carry out my life having faith and strength to overcome the obstacles I have been unable to in the past.

 To step out in full faith for my spirit to use me to illustrated itself.

 To live like I want to live, rather than living like I think I have to...

 And it seems like I am enjoying this sketching more than I thought I would. Not a bad day :)

Lessons Learned in Life: Day 12 of 30-Day Reprieve... Expectations

Difference between needs and expectations.

A need will always carry with it added value. Expectations assist in covering up something within myself.

As I am proceeding though this journey it seems I come up against my expectations quite often. The statement above is helping me immensely...

Also, I am realizing my 'needs' are so few compared to what my mind tells me they are...

Lessons Learned in Life: Day 13 of 30-Day Reprieve... Compassion

Day 13!! *Woo-Hoo!* I am still surviving; I haven't gone completely mad or hurt myself or anyone else...lol

Although I feel like I still have some struggle in being present, I seem to be getting more comfortable with entertaining myself, by selecting how I want to spend my time, rather than a TV show or other activity. One of the things I haven't mentioned before (I think), is how I have viewed television for a while now.

I am not sure where I developed this thought, but watching the tube for me, is watching other people live out their passion.

Today, the word compassion seemed to keep coming up throughout my day. I realized that there was a long time in my life I confused compassion with "caving in." More recently I stopped showing compassion to break the link to caving in. Today, I seem to focus more on being able to show compassion, without picking up whatever it is being discussed. Not always an easy thing. Partially because I'm a male, so I carry the fix-it gene in me, but also because I

Do not likely see someone I care about struggle or bothered.

Ultimately, I had to learn how to let other people have their feelings of disappointment. Be able to listen to them without sacrificing myself.

Self-sacrificing is all about going against what is best for me in order to please someone else...

daba daba dats all folks!

Lessons Learned in Life: Day 21 of 30-Day Reprieve... Grieving

There seems to be something taking root through this process...

So far, in twenty-one (21) days, I have taken up drawing, have become much more confident in the work I do, have been asked to start writing a book, based in my blog, have moved forward with the love of my life and moving in together.

Those are the exterior changes that have come about or strengthened in this past twenty-one (21) days! From the interior, I am learning to sit alone, without outside influence for longer periods of time than I have been capable of doing so at this point. I have had to find new ways to pick my spirits up from being depressed, or make contact with someone to do so, in place of utilizing the TV, music or reading.

It turns out the drawing process has assisted me in processing through the sadness of my Mom passing. I was trying to draw a portrait of her, for no other reason than I wanted to. I tried to do so three (3) times one evening and each time I could not put two lines together without ripping the page out and starting over.

The next day I realized that these drawings are surfacing thorough a meditative process.

Since I am still grieving her passing, there is naturally a block with every time I try to draw her. This block allows me to process the emotions and when the time is right, I'll complete that sketch!!

Lessons Learned in Life: Day 30 of 30-Day Reprieve: Wrap Up

 So here I sit thirty (30) days later. Am I changed? Did I obtain enlightenment? Will the remainder of my life be different as a result of this challenge?

 These were the expectations I think I set for myself going in, for example, I wanted my experience to be similar to a spiritual master spending year in the mountains becoming enlightened. And of course, I would… why wouldn't I!!

 What I did learn in my thirty (30) day experiment was how to be more active in my life. Here are some of the experiences I encountered… I traveled to Utah (more specifically Moab) where we were able to hike at night without flashlights. First time I hiked by the light of the moon… AWESOME!
Campfires at my property in Iowa, hiked sand dunes in Michigan, with my little buddy.

 Maybe not so smart while in rehab for shoulder when I was forced to crabwalk up with him on my back, but still a great memory. Thanks to an invite from a friend, I was able to be at Lambeau Field when the Detroit Lions broke a twenty-four (24) year losing streak. Reconnected with friends, enjoyed the new Rocky movie with my baby, my son and his buddy, and a trip to Arizona.

During this past thirty (30) days, I learned I am able to sketch what I would have described as my skill level. Along with this, I learned that sketching carries a large degree of solitude. It is meditative to sit down with a pencil and paper and sketch. I found my mind didn't wonder as I did so.

I found out how much I appreciate music, and I really missed it. I did not realize it fully until I was at physical therapy and they had the radio playing. I could have stayed there all day!!

I spent a fair amount of time being bored; in the past I would have grabbed the remote, a book or something to break the boredom. I was forced to make a selection that involved me. There was always an easy choice, but I didn't always choose the healthiest choice.

I learned that grieving takes what it takes. I thought I allowed myself enough time to grieve the passing of my Mom. The harder I worked at forcing the conclusion the stronger my feelings

wanted a distraction. Additionally, I learned whenever I am reaching for a distraction, it is to avoid something. There is a difference between choosing an activity and choosing an activity to avoid something else. It is not always easy to see when in the midst of it. To avoid something means to me whatever I select to put in place of it will not be a healthy choice. I am not sure of anyone else, but I have never grabbed carrots as a distraction.
Sounds simplistic, but in application, not always easy to recognize.

Looking back, the one thing I wish I had more of, during this thirty (30) day period is structure. I realize now, but having additional structure, such as meditation time, writing time...

I think I would have received additional insights. Not that I am complaining! What I am is moving into Phase II. A twenty-one (21) day cleanse in up and coming with a 'lil more wisdom, structure and willingness to be open to the lessons that unfold!!

Conclusion

Let me start by saying a sincere, deep felt "Thank You!" I am amazed that my life has brought me to the point of authoring this book, and I am truly grateful you chose to read it. I hope you enjoyed the experience and my greatest wish is that something in these pages has touched you or sparked a thought within your soul of its existence and its passion to be a larger part of your everyday life.

The intent of publishing was to share how one man's life has changed, once he started paying attention to the events that unfolded through his day, in order to maybe bring a flicker of light into someone doing the same in their life.

It has been amazing so far and I assume life will continue to bring understanding, enlightenment and the WOW factor into the days, weeks, months and years ahead!!

My greatest passion is to build an ever-expanding community from all walks of life, who are searching for the answers to what I call "the big reason" why events, people and things appear in our lives. Each decision we face is a Life's-lesson and it really is all about steering life into being fuller, more beautiful and self-driven.

 In moving forward, I am available for discussion, coaching, or speaking and can be reached at any of the following locations...

www.lifes-lessons.com

Facebook: Joseph A.

Droshagen

Twitter: Lifeslessons00

Email: ifgtcoahcing@gmail.com

May you dive deeply into your Life's-lessons and discover all that you are!

Namaste,

Joseph

58992894R00111

Made in the USA
Columbia, SC
03 June 2019